Outback
Midwife

Outback Midwife

BETH McRAE

WITH CHARLOTTE WARD

BANTAM

SYDNEY AUCKLAND TORONTO NEW YORK LONDON

A Bantam book
Published by Random House Australia Pty Ltd
Level 3, 100 Pacific Highway, North Sydney NSW 2060
www.randomhouse.com.au

Penguin
Random House
RANDOM HOUSE BOOKS

First published by Bantam in 2015

Copyright © Elizabeth McRae and Charlotte Ward 2015

The moral right of the authors has been asserted.

Random House Books is part of the Penguin Random House group of companies
whose addresses can be found at global.penguinrandomhouse.com.

National Library of Australia
Cataloguing-in-Publication Entry

McRae, Beth, author
Outback midwife / Beth McRae
9780857983947 (paperback)
McRae, Beth
Midwives – Australia Biography
Country life – Australia
618.20092

Cover photographs courtesy of Trevillion Images and Getty Images (mother and child)
Cover design by Christabella Designs
Internal design by Midland Typesetters, Ausralia
Typeset in 13/18 pt Adobe Garamond LT by Midland Typesetters, Australia
Printed in Australia by Griffin Press, an accredited ISO AS/NZS 14001:2004
Environmental Management System printer

Random House Australia uses papers that are natural, renewable and recyclable
products and made from wood grown in sustainable forests. The logging and
manufacturing processes are expected to conform to the environmental
regulations of the country of origin.

Contents

I would like to dedicate this book to remote health workers everywhere – your expertise and experience are invaluable and it has been a privilege to have worked among you.

Author's Note

In order to maintain the necessary confidentiality of the women, doctors, nurses and hospitals in the book, some of the characters described are amalgams of two or more people, and have been given pseudonyms; however, all the stories I have told occurred in one form or another. They are occurring every day in our hospitals and outback communities.

Prologue

Mesmerised, I watched as Margaret, a white-haired Aboriginal elder, sat cross-legged on the ground and gently laid the baby in her arms onto warm, fire-heated sand. As smoke from the nearby fire wafted over them, Margaret cradled the baby's head with one hand and used the other to sprinkle clean sand on to his naked body. Although her two-week-old great-grandson wriggled a little at the new sensation, he didn't cry. Instead, his gaze rested on his elderly relative, his big brown eyes blinking in the flickering firelight.

There was nothing grand about this ritual, which took place in the family's backyard, and no special ceremonial words were spoken. But as I sat on the ground next to Margaret and her granddaughter, Leona, the baby's mother, I felt privileged to be witnessing such an intimate moment.

I'd come to know Margaret and Leona well during the seven months they'd been visiting me at the health clinic. At 19, Leona was a young mother and she'd needed special attention in the lead-up to giving birth. Having been diagnosed with rheumatic heart disease when she was 15, Leona needed monthly injections of penicillin. So during her pregnancy I'd been administering the injections for her heart condition, and keeping a close eye on her.

After Leona's mother had died a few years earlier, she had begun to rely on her grandmother and she would often arrive at the clinic with her in tow. Margaret clearly loved her granddaughter very much and it was touching to see how attentive and supportive she was in helping Leona through her first experience of pregnancy.

Thankfully, she advanced into her third trimester with few problems, and when she reached 36 weeks I arranged for her to be flown to Darwin to give birth at the hospital there. Given her heart condition, every precaution had to be taken; therefore she would be induced so that when she went into labour she could be closely monitored by obstetricians and cardiac doctors on duty at the hospital, rather than at night when they might not be there.

Two weeks later I was thrilled to hear that Leona had safely delivered her baby boy, Jarrah, and would be flying back to the community in a few days. It wasn't long before she and Margaret arrived at the clinic, both smiling widely and eager to show off the gorgeous curly-haired bub in Leona's arms.

'We're doing the smoking ceremony tonight,' Margaret told me. 'Will you come?'

I was barely able to contain my surprise and delight. I'd heard a little about Aboriginal smoking ceremonies, a traditional rite of passage carried out to ensure babies begin life knowing where they come from and where they belong. It was a ceremony for women only – 'women's business' – and a part of Aboriginal culture that has been passed down through the generations. I'd certainly never expected to be invited to one.

Arriving at Margaret and Leona's home that evening, I clutched the scones I'd baked, hoping they were a suitable gift. Feeling nervous I might be intruding, I was ready to make my excuses if my presence there seemed inappropriate. But they greeted me warmly and ushered me into the backyard. I'd expected to find a huddle of female relatives, but as Leona beckoned for me to join her on the ground next to a campfire, I was surprised to see that baby Jarrah would experience this important rite of passage with just the three of us.

Crouching down to sit next to Leona, I watched as she cooed over her baby. Meanwhile Margaret busied herself stoking the fire of wood and leaves she'd set to warm the sand collected from a local beach. It felt very peaceful as the sound of Jarrah's soft gurgles mingled with the gentle crackle and pop of the fire, the melodic hum of the night critters, distant barks of dogs, and tinny music drifting over this balmy evening.

Margaret made sure the sand was clean and not too hot by picking out any small pieces of charcoal before she sprinkled the grains on to the baby's skin. After gently dusting Jarrah's torso, she turned him over, carefully resting him across her left arm as she used her right hand to shower his back with the warm, fine granules.

'Now he knows his land and where he comes from,' Leona whispered to me.

We watched as Margaret placed the baby onto her lap, warmed her hands in the smoke and rubbed them gently over Jarrah's skin. 'To help him grow strong without sickness,' Leona said.

Lastly, standing slowly, Margaret lifted Jarrah through the smoke before she returned him to his mother's arms. This would be the first of many times throughout his life that the young boy would be smoked, to help him stay connected to the land and to ensure good health and strength.

'Did you enjoy it?' Margaret asked me, with a wide smile.

'It was pretty special,' I said, feeling a little overwhelmed. Suddenly I remembered to hand Margaret the container of scones I was still holding. I'd thought they'd probably boil the billy and have a cuppa now, but I felt I'd invaded their family time enough. So, after thanking them and giving baby Jarrah a last cuddle, I made for home, gripping the big stick I always carried to ward off the packs of dogs I might meet en route.

Walking the short journey home along roads in varying degrees of disrepair, I passed the metal-framed houses characteristic of the community, my heart lifting when occasionally a mum I'd cared for called out a greeting, 'Hello, Pet!'

PROLOGUE

Before coming to Maningrida, an Aboriginal town in the heart of Arnhem Land, I'd had no idea whether I'd hack it living and working in the outback. It hadn't been easy taking a leap of faith, leaving my daughters and grand-children behind and giving up everything to move to the Northern Territory.

Living in Maningrida had proved every bit as over-whelming and tough as I'd expected, but on magical evenings like this I was reminded of all the reasons why I'd chosen to take on the biggest challenge of my career – working as a remote area midwife.

Chapter 1
Maybe, baby

Riding across the bumpy paddock in Dad's Land Rover, I gripped hold of the seat and pushed my wind-lashed hair from my eyes as I searched the field for newborn calves. We soon came upon several, watching us with big brown eyes and taking wobbly steps to stay close to their mothers. I spotted a cow licking a newborn calf yet to find its feet, and was alarmed to see a thick, silvery-looking substance hanging from under the cow's tail.

'What's that slimy stuff?' I asked. 'Is there something wrong with her?'

'She's just had a calf, Beth,' Dad said brusquely. Before I had a chance to ask any more questions, he did a quick about-turn and dropped me back at the house.

As a tomboyish and curious nine-year-old, I often accompanied Dad on his rounds of our 3000-acre cattle farm in Cudgewa, a small country town at the north-eastern tip of Victoria. Cudgewa was an archetypal bush town: its population was under 300; it had one pub, a post office, a general store, a two-teacher school and, like many small country towns, a local Mechanics' Institute, which was the hub for all important community events. The nearest large town was Corryong, about 10 kilometres from the New South Wales border.

Although Dad taught me lots of things, like how to bottle-feed orphan calves, trap and skin rabbits, and 'turn the churn' in the separating room where we skimmed the milk and cream, the birds and the bees were not up for discussion. My parents were conservative people who had no intention of enlightening their two daughters about sex. My older sister, Faye, and I weren't even allowed to attend sex education classes at school, so the little I eventually learnt about 'doing it' was gleaned from other 11-year-olds in hushed tones during horticulture classes in the school garden. When my period arrived, a week after my 12th birthday, Mum seemed embarrassed. 'I meant to tell you about that,' she said unconvincingly. But we never did have 'the talk'. It was only when I was 15 and one of the senior students fell pregnant amid much schoolyard scandal that I heard an anatomical description of how babies were made. I often think it's a shame Dad didn't let me help with the calving as it would have been a good introduction to the facts of life, not to mention midwifery. To this day, watching animals in labour is always a great reminder to me of how natural a process birthing is.

While the details of our conceptions remained a taboo subject, Mum did eventually tell Faye and me a little about our own births. Faye had made her entrance in the breech position (legs first), surprising everyone and creating a medical emergency. Faye's awkward positioning caused Mum great difficulty in labour and eventually the doctor had to sedate her while he and a midwife wrestled the baby out. Horrifically, both Faye's legs were broken in the process.

'You had your legs in plaster for the first three weeks of your life,' Mum told a wide-eyed Faye.

Understandably, Mum was nervous about my birth, but unlike my sister apparently I couldn't wait to get out. When my mother arrived at the hospital with ruptured membranes but no pain other than a slightly uncomfortable feeling, she was instructed to rest on a chair in the ward while the midwife fetched her paperwork. It was only when Mum felt a searing contraction and the sudden urge to push that she realised my birth was imminent.

'You just fell out,' she said.

Growing up on a farm was a great life for a tomboy, and I spent every spare moment playing outside, climbing trees or hurtling along the dusty country roads on my second-hand bike. Like most siblings so close in age (there were 14 months between us) Faye and I veered between blissful

8

sisterly moments, swimming in the creek or playing tennis, and all-out war, with ferocious fights over games of Snakes and Ladders.

We'd heard enviable stories of friends left home alone unsupervised while their parents went to the pub, but Faye and I spent our Saturday nights at the local hall, where Mum and Dad helped host dances to raise money for good causes such as the upkeep of the football club. This clean-cut family fun suited my parents, who didn't smoke or drink and frowned upon people who did.

At 6 pm Dad would take the money on the door and the locals would spill through to do the foxtrot, one step and the Pride of Erin, swirling and sliding around the wooden floor with ease, thanks to the pallet wax Dad had spread earlier. Faye and I loved to watch and this is how we learnt to dance, implicitly putting aside our adolescent differences to hop and skip backwards and forwards to the progressive barn dance.

As we navigated our teenage years, Faye became a terrible dobber. Whether I'd used Dad's razor to shave my legs or sat giggling next to a boy on the school bus, she would inevitably go racing off to Mum to tell all. Never mind that Miss Goody-Two-Shoes herself had been dating a local boy, Paul, since she'd turned 12. Regardless, Mum, who was the boss of the household, would chastise me for 'trying to grow up too fast'. With our set bedtime of 9 pm and compulsory Sunday School every weekend, there didn't seem much chance of that!

My first taste of freedom came at the end of 1968, when Faye left school (and home) to work as a receptionist at the local hospital in Corryong, where we were both born. My parents, keen to keep a watchful eye on her romance with Paul, immediately set her up with lodgings at the home of family friends. Meanwhile I celebrated the fact that I finally had the bathroom to myself in the morning and no prying sister to spy on me.

I was 16 and just one school year behind Faye, so soon I too would need to think about a career. Although I was bright enough to pass most of my subjects, I was a bit clueless as to what I should do next. Girls at my country school in the 1960s had limited career options and were encouraged to pursue safe womanly pursuits such as secretarial work, nursing, teaching or hairdressing.

My teacher reported, 'I would suggest that any position where it is possible for Beth to deal with people would be an ideal situation, as her friendliness and open personality are assets that could be well used.' I toyed with the idea of becoming a teacher. But I also liked the idea of nursing. Often, after tea, we'd watch the American medical drama *Ben Casey*. Dr Casey was constantly surrounded by a gaggle of glamorous nurses, who spent their time caring for and chatting to patients. It looked like an interesting job for someone like me, who was always getting told off in class for talking. And, having helped Dad slaughter sheep on the farm, I definitely wasn't squeamish about blood.

'Nursing would be a very good thing for you to do,' Mum agreed when we discussed it. 'It suits your personality – you're very practical.'

'Plus you can look after us in our old age,' Dad laughed.

Being naturally adventurous, I thought it was absolutely worth exploring as an escape route, having cottoned on to the fact that there were nursing schools all over the country to choose from. The idea of getting away appealed to me, and after studying the many adverts for nursing vacancies, I had my future all plotted out. I'd apply to Preston and Northcote Community Hospital (PANCH), which was over 400 kilometres away in Melbourne. Freedom beckoned.

'It's got a good reputation and great facilities,' I told Mum and Dad. I didn't let on that by 'facilities' I meant the nurses' home swimming pool described in the advert.

'What about Albury?' Mum said. 'That's much closer.'

Albury, a little more than 100 kilometres over the border in New South Wales, represented the youthful independence that Mum had never quite achieved. It was where she had gone to boarding school, and as a teenager she'd planned to stay in the city and get a job in a shop. But when her parents died within two years of each other, her grandfather summoned her back to the farm. In his mind it wasn't proper for a 17-year-old girl to work outside the home if her parents weren't around to pay her keep. By the time Mum was 18 she had succumbed to convention, marrying Wallace the farmhand (my dad), and baby Faye was on the way. Although Mum was in love and wanted to marry Dad,

I think she would have liked to have lived a little more of her own life first.

Sensing my lack of interest, my parents tried a different approach – bribery. 'If you do your nursing in Albury, we'll buy you a car so you can come home on your days off,' Dad said. Well, that sold it for me. Having my own car would give me freedom, and, after all, 117 kilometres was still a fair distance from home.

My interview at Albury Base Hospital in September 1969 was surprisingly informal. It turned out that the matron, a 40-something woman who wore a huge sister's veil (or 'flying nun headpiece' as we called it behind her back) and my parents had friends in common so we chatted about a well-to-do family we both knew in Cudgewa. Perhaps she assumed I was posh by association because she offered me a place as a student nurse on the spot, starting in July 1970 with a wage of $48 a fortnight. Whatever her reasons for giving me this opportunity out of the blue, favouritism based on connections was not uncommon in country communities at the time, and I was just happy I'd managed to slip into the position.

With everything in place, I finished school in December 1969 and started a six-month stint working in a clothes shop in Corryong to tide me over until July. By now I had my first boyfriend, a lad called Kevin who lived up the road and worked on his parents' farm with his two older brothers. Kevin was well built with longish hair like David Bowie. He was a very good footballer and often drove to Albury to go to training. I had high hopes our romance would last, despite the distance.

On a cold day in July 1970 – a month before my 18th birthday – my parents and I set off on the 90-minute drive to the red-brick nurses' home at Albury Base Hospital. As Dad carried my large suitcase up the draughty staircase, he paused and looked back at me. 'It's too cold to start nursing now,' he said. 'Why don't you wait until it gets warmer?'

Although he was smiling, I knew that was Dad's way of telling me he felt sad I was leaving home. I was the closest thing he had to a son and I think he would've been happy if I'd decided to stay on the farm working with him.

Finding the small room I'd been allocated, I opened the door to see the single bed was already occupied by a long-limbed, dark-haired girl. Glancing up from reading, she introduced herself as Pam.

I walked through a large double-hung window and found my bed – on the chilly, enclosed verandah. 'Will you be warm enough?' Mum asked. I could see there was limited heating, and the accommodation was hardly luxurious. 'It's fine,' I insisted, smiling at my roommate.

Bidding my parents goodbye, I began to unpack my belongings into a bedside locker and the double wardrobe I'd be sharing with Pam. It didn't take long for us to break the ice. Just like me, she was a farmer's daughter who'd never lived away from home before. Excited by our new-found freedom, and feeling already as though we'd be good friends, we headed across the road to buy cigarettes. My parents certainly wouldn't have approved, but I'd started to have the odd sneaky cigarette when I was working in Corryong and saw them as the height of cool and sophistication, of course blissfully unaware of their health risks.

Back in our room, we were interrupted by a knock on the door. I opened it to find a young woman in a white sister's uniform. 'Here,' she said, handing over two plastic containers. 'Don't forget to bring your urine sample tomorrow.' She didn't explain why and I was too timid to ask.

The following morning, with our samples sloshing around in our pockets, Pam and I put on our matching homemade blue starched uniforms (the material and pattern had been sent in the mail and stitched by our mums) and crossed the hospital grounds to the shabby, heritage-listed building that housed the nursing school. We headed up a rickety staircase at the back of the building. For the first six weeks our lessons would take place in a cold, damp classroom, with only occasional visits to the hospital.

Our class of five students would be shown the ropes by Sister Alberts, a petite woman in her 50s whose huge veil almost eclipsed her. After checking the cleanliness of our fingernails, she summoned us to form a circle around an old hospital bed. Lying on the mattress was Mrs McTavish, an ugly plastic dummy that looked a bit like the blow-up dolls you see in sex shops, but without the lipstick!

'I'm going to demonstrate how to carry out a bed bath,' she said. Taking a sponge, Sister Alberts wiped the dummy's face, then moved down the body, washing the doll's intimate areas last. Next, she taught us the correct way to make a bed, explaining how the sheets and blankets should be tucked in perfectly straight lines along the edges of the bed, with no wrinkles on the top, and finished off with the all-important mitred (squared-off) corners.

I thought it was strange she hadn't asked for our urine samples. It was only that evening, when the 'sister' revealed her true identity as a student nurse from the year above, that we realised we'd been had in a traditional nurses' home initiation.

Less amusing was the note I found in my room reminding me to make my bed properly. My sloppy efforts that morning had been torn apart by the real sister in charge of the nurses' home. I quickly realised that the regimented bed-making technique I'd learnt in the classroom applied to our lodgings as well and our bedroom would be inspected daily.

During the next few weeks Pam and I honed our skills in bandaging, bed-pan cleaning and linen folding. We were also taught the art of changing bedding with a patient still in the bed – by manhandling Mrs McTavish from left to right as we refreshed the sheets in double-quick time. With everything done under Sister Alberts's watchful eye, there was no giggling or messing about – she'd warned us that 'nursing etiquette' should be adhered to at all times. Whenever she or a senior member of staff addressed us, we were to stand silently with our hands behind our backs. Likewise, as lowly student nurses we should always be the last member of staff to walk into a room. This hierarchy also applied to the nurses' home, where it was our duty to answer the phone and front door and seek out the person needed.

We were also at the beck and call of the second- and third-year students, who were known to take advantage. The less pleasant jobs offloaded to us included scrubbing and sterilising the stainless steel bed pans, vomit bowls and urinals. It was not wise to complain to a senior about these jobs, so we extracted our revenge via more crafty means. It was funny how often a boyfriend or suitor could call the nurses' home and have their message 'accidentally' mislaid.

In September 1970, after six weeks at Preliminary Training School covering the theory of nursing, I was allocated my first ward, Blackie B – a private medical and surgical ward where I would learn the ropes for six weeks. My mentor was a senior nurse called Jeanette, who was very nice to me. It was under her watchful eye that I performed my first procedure, removing a man's abdominal stitches with sterilised tweezers and scissors. Following her instructions to 'lift the stitch and cut under the knot', I carefully pulled away the blood-crusted thread and was thrilled to be praised by my patient for my gentleness. 'I wouldn't have known it was your first time,' he told me.

With bed baths, bed pans and bed-wetting an everyday part of life on the ward, there was no avoiding the intimate nature of nursing. I was grateful for the male orderlies who assisted male patients with personal hygiene and preparation for theatre, which often included a nipple-to-knee shave if they were having abdominal surgery.

However, one evening, as I worked a late shift, a 17-year-old teenager was admitted with appendicitis. He was scheduled for an emergency appendectomy, and with no orderlies available it was my job to shave him. The thought of shaving a man 'down there' was terrifying, but I gritted my teeth and discreetly covered his private parts with a towel, gently pushing his penis to one side and then the other while I shaved his groin. We were both aware of his body reacting.

'I think it can hold itself up now, nurse,' he said, clearly mortified. I quickly finished the job, feeling my own cheeks heating up with embarrassment, and left him to dress himself in his theatre gown.

'It happens,' Jeanette laughed when I told her the next day. 'Just don't tell your boyfriend!'

Day to day I loved the camaraderie of living with a bunch of girls my own age, despite having to go to bed in a woolly hat and thick socks when the temperature dropped to freezing, a little too often for my liking. Pam and I were fast becoming best friends, with nightly debriefs in our room as we shared stories and gossip from our days on the ward. Whenever she had a day off, Pam would head home to Corowa, on the New South Wales side of the border, to see her boyfriend,

George. Sometimes George would drive to Albury and we'd all go for drinks at the Albion, the pub closest to the nurses' home, where we could let off steam after a hard day with the bed pans.

Despite Kevin's constant travel back and forth to football training in Albury, in three months he still hadn't shown his face. 'Are you sure he really exists?' Pam teased one day.

'Yes,' I scowled, tossing a pillow at her. 'I saw him last weekend.' I'd called to see Kevin in my new white four-door Cortina while home in Cudgewa, and it was irritating that he hadn't returned the courtesy or made any effort to see me.

My next rotation was working night duty in a ward for elderly women who were suffering from dementia or needed constant nursing care. The ward was quiet at night so to stay awake I would kill time studying or smoking at the nurses' desk. I know! But in those days it was perfectly acceptable to smoke anywhere in the hospital and I would often puff through a packet as I read my textbooks.

Although a relief nurse came in twice during the night, primarily to help me change wet beds, I spent the majority of my shift on my own in the dimly lit ward. This could be creepy, especially as we were right next to the morgue. If I heard the sound of trolley wheels on the concrete I knew there had been a death, and the thought always made me shudder.

At this point I hadn't yet seen a dead body – that came later when I was working on the male medical ward – but more than once I wondered if an elderly patient had passed away on my shift. Some old ladies were so deathly still while they slept that I'd have to creep really close to check they were breathing. And of course I had to be as deathly silent so as not to wake them and scare them silly.

The morning staff arrived at 6.30, expecting the most fragile, bed-bound patients to be washed and their linen changed. This meant waking the weakest and often sleepiest patients at 4 am and subjecting them to bed baths. It seemed common sense to me that sick people should be allowed to sleep, and I hated enforcing a procedure that struck me as cruel for the sake of someone else's convenience, but this kind of thing was commonplace in hospitals in those days – often patients didn't come first, hospital routines did.

One of the most talked-about rotations was the emergency department, where students were warned to expect the unexpected, administering to gruesome accidents, broken bones and coming face to face with literal blood and gore. While some student nurses seemed to be what we called 'shit magnets' – attracting multiple car pile-ups, chest-pain sufferers, snakebite victims, near-drownings and stab wounds during their shifts – at first I had it easy during my rotation. One week in, my biggest drama had been a local school caretaker who'd smashed his thumb with a hammer.

So I was feeling fairly smug, and vastly relieved, until I was called to assist with a man with suspected meningitis. In order to be sure of his diagnosis, the doctor needed to do a lumber puncture procedure to extract the patient's spine fluid for testing. The man sat straddled across a chair while a doctor took a five-inch needle and began to push it between his vertebrae. It was my job to hold out the specimen-collecting tubes without touching the doctor. It was a tricky and painful procedure so the atmosphere was unbearably tense. I couldn't help putting myself in the man's position and imagining how terrifying and painful this would be.

Suddenly I began to feel unsteady on my legs and sick in my stomach. Forcing myself to take deep, steady breaths, I managed to keep focused until it was all over. Then, making my excuses, I staggered outside to sit on a bench, taking big gulps of fresh air to collect myself. I have never fainted before or since, but that day I was very close to face-planting the floor.

The army camp Bandiana was only 13 kilometres from Albury Hospital, and it was not unusual for plucky young men to phone the nurses' home fishing for dates. If they hadn't been told to come to the door and ask for 'Melina Stool' (the medical term for blood in faeces), they could usually secure some female company for the evening on turning up at the home. A few of my friends were dating army lads from the camp, so one February night after finishing a busy 10 am to 6.30 pm shift on the Children's Ward I headed to another of our haunts, the Globe Hotel, to join them.

In the dimly lit pub, I spotted my friends crowded around a long wooden table. The only space was next to a skinny blond guy. 'Here's one for you, Macca,' I heard the lad next to him whisper.

'What about some introductions?' the skinny private said. 'I'm Ian. This lot call me Macca.'

Ian, who told me he was training to be an army mechanic, was 17 – seven months younger than me. Pam and I laughed a lot with those boys that night, and I was pleased to find out that Ian wanted to see me again. He'd paid for my drinks and been very much a gentleman, acknowledging our presence by standing whenever we came to the table. With the lesser-spotted Kevin still apparently reluctant to visit me, I enjoyed the attention and didn't feel guilty about agreeing to a date.

The following Wednesday evening I met Ian in the lobby of the nurses' home, hoping to make an impression with my new snakeskin print mini dress. Ian didn't have a car so I drove us to a bar called the Camelot Lounge where the music wasn't too loud and we could talk. He told me he was from the Upper Murray in South Australia, where his family farmed a 26-acre fruit block. As we talked, I remember thinking he was such a refreshing change from the stolid farm boys I'd gone to school with. The way he told his stories about life in the army was so funny and mischievous, and I couldn't help being attracted to his obvious sense of adventure and can-do attitude.

Unlike Kevin, Ian was more than eager to call at the nurses' home, and after that we went out most weeks – dancing at pubs where live bands played, or canoodling at drive-in movies.

After a couple of months we had become so close I knew this was serious, so as soon as I had a weekend off, I invited

Ian home to Cudgewa to meet my parents. I really wanted to share my home with Ian, and knowing he was a country boy I thought he'd enjoy it. Ian was a great shot – as you'd expect from someone in the army – and he was looking forward to going 'spotlighting' with Dad – night-shooting foxes, rabbits and kangaroos, which farmers like my dad considered feral animals that damaged their livelihoods and needed constant culling to keep under control.

I had high hopes my parents would like Ian. However, things got off to a bad start that weekend. My father, who believed men on farms should rise early to help, looked far from pleased when Ian still hadn't surfaced at 11 the next morning. He wasn't to know that Ian had been on guard duty two nights before, working two hours on and two hours off. I tried explaining this to Dad, but he was having none of it.

'Blokes like you are meant to be protecting our country,' he muttered when Ian finally appeared. 'You can't sleep all day.'

And Dad wasn't the only one whose nose was put out of joint. The following week I received a call from a distraught Kevin, who'd heard on the grapevine I'd been seen driving through the town with 'another fella'.

'What did I do?' he asked.

'It's what you didn't do. You could never be bothered to come and visit me,' I said. 'So I found someone who would.'

Chapter 2
Yes, matron

Leaning back on my deckchair under the shade of the maple tree, I closed my eyes, enjoying the kookaburra chorus. A couple of days back at home with Mum and Dad were always a welcome retreat from my busy life at the hospital. Inside the house I could hear Mum banging around and muttering to herself as she went about her usual morning chores.

When the phone rang, I heard her say, 'Hold on, I'll just get her.' She called from the kitchen window, 'It's your sister. She says there's an emergency at Corryong.'

Faye sounded stressed. She quickly explained that 25 schoolchildren had been in a bus accident in Khancoban, a small country town 27 kilometres away on the western slopes of the Snowy Mountains, where the roads could be treacherous. Corryong Hospital, where Faye worked, was nearest to the scene so all the injured children were being taken there. The staff were getting ready to deal with the influx and, being a small rural hospital, they needed as much help as they could muster.

'I'll leave now,' I promised, hanging up the phone and heading into my bedroom. I didn't have my nurse's uniform with me so I changed into the first light-coloured dress I could find and a pair of flat shoes.

I rushed off to the hospital, my stomach churning. I was four months into my second year of nursing but I'd never been called out to an emergency situation before and I wondered what I would find. Hurrying into the front foyer of the hospital, I spotted Faye, who led me past the reception area to the small emergency department. It was already chaotic. Pale, frightened teenage girls were sobbing, swapping stories while a frazzled-looking nurse tried to extract their parents' contact numbers from them.

Eunice, the hospital's charge sister, was attending to a woman on a trolley who had a mangled-looking leg. The patient was wearing a nun's habit and was holding an oxygen mask to her face. 'Get Sister Celia in the ambulance to Albury,' I heard Eunice say to a hovering porter.

'Beth's here to help,' Faye told a colleague. 'What do you want her to do?'

Eunice led me into the patients' sitting room, in which the furniture had been pushed to one side. Four portable beds had been set up to create a makeshift observation ward and each one was occupied by a Year 9 student from the bus crash.

'Can you stay here and take their vitals every hour?' Eunice asked, quickly introducing me to each of my young patients. Justine had a nasty gash across her forehead and was waiting to have stitches; Lizzie was resting after being badly shaken; Becky had her arm in a sling; and Annie had knocked her head and was developing black eyes.

'I won't have time to check on you, so you'll need to send for someone if there are any changes,' she said.

With that, she disappeared. While I was familiar with the observations for head injuries, I'd never had this much responsibility before, and I was both frightened and flattered that Eunice had spoken to me as if I were a senior nurse. Aware that my patients were now looking at me expectantly, I smiled in the hope of appearing experienced and in control.

Surveying the room, I checked what equipment I had. There was a blood-pressure machine, a thermometer and a pen torch. Beginning with Justine, I checked her wound and shone the torch into her eyes. I carefully ran through the 'head injuries checklist' I'd learnt in class, and noted that her pupils were the same size and reacting to light as they should be. Next, I asked her to squeeze both her hands, wiggle her toes and tell me what day it was. So far, so good.

Placing Justine's left arm into the cuff of the blood-pressure machine, I double-checked the reading. It was normal so I jotted it down on the patient's chart and measured her pulse and temperature, relieved that they were also fine. Taking my watch, I waited for a minute, counting the rise and fall in her chest. This confirmed to me that Justine was breathing at a normal rate.

As I repeated these checks from bed to bed, the class-mates seemed keen to tell me what had happened, recalling with wide eyes exactly what they'd been doing and thinking as their bus had slid off the mountain road, plummeted downhill and slammed into a tree. I knew the steep, winding road where the accident had happened and it sounded as though they'd had a lucky escape. If the bus had rolled, they would likely have all been killed.

Despite their ordeal, the girls slowly began to perk up, embracing the collective camaraderie of surviving a near-death experience, and their chatter helped to calm me too.

I'd been at the hospital for eight hours when Eunice returned to tell me I could go home. She and her team had been flat out, dealing with broken arms, legs and ankles, as well as minor bruises, cuts and scratches. Two teachers with more serious injuries, including the nun I'd seen earlier, had been transferred to my hospital in Albury. With extra night staff drafted in and parents arriving from Melbourne to collect their daughters, everything was now under control.

Driving back to the nurses' home after the unexpected drama of my day off, I felt exhilarated. Just like the girls in my care, I'd survived my first crisis. Being at the bottom of the hospital food chain as a student nurse, I was used to being constantly monitored and checked, so Eunice's faith in my ability to cope by myself had given me confidence. I'd loved the responsibility, making myself useful and being able to rally so well in an emergency situation I'd had little real experience of.

Now I'd begun my second year at Albury, I had two stripes stitched into my nursing cap and it was my job to supervise the new nurses on the general wards. Of course, we carried out our own silly initiations on the juniors (including sending them to the sterilising department to ask for a pair of fallopian tubes), but essentially we were expected to organise them in keeping the wards tidy and dealing with patient hygiene. In between, we would administer medication, take patients to and from theatre and change complicated dressings, painstakingly removing dead skin or probing into nasty wounds so that the tissue could repair without infection.

As busy as I was, Ian was still very much on the scene, despite having been transferred 368 kilometres away to Puckapunyal army barracks near Melbourne in August 1971. He travelled to Albury most weekends, getting a lift from mates who were also visiting girlfriends or family in the area. Most Saturday nights we would spend the evening smooching at the Horseshoe Lagoon or cuddling up on East Albury Hill, enjoying the twinkling lights of the city and the view of Monument Hill.

As a second year I now had my own room. However, unfortunately for Ian, overnight visitors at the nurses' home were strictly prohibited. Any nurse caught with a male guest in her room would be instantly dismissed. While I retired sheepishly to my bed, Ian, a lanky 5 foot 10, was forced to bunk down with a sleeping bag and pillow on the cramped back seat of my Cortina. On the nights when I missed my midnight curfew and found the doors of the nurses' home were bolted, I'd squeeze onto the back seat as well. Somehow the two of us would manage to sleep in a spooning position, me with my knees wedged up against the front seat. Then I had to hope there wouldn't be a bed check – when the night-duty supervisor could be bothered, she would check our rooms to see we were all where we should be. Luckily, I was never caught.

On my weekends off, Ian would come home with me to Cudgewa. There, he had the luxury of sleeping inside a house, but he was not allowed into my bedroom – under *any* circumstances. Ian found this out the hard way when, one Saturday morning, Mum walked in to find him sitting on the edge of my bed chatting to me.

'Get out of that bed!' she screamed, quickly backing out of the room. She seemed oblivious to the fact that Ian was not, in fact, in my bed, that he was fully dressed and that I was innocently in my pyjamas under the covers. It was like she'd caught us having sex, and unfortunately yet another reason to dislike Ian.

I'd been dating Ian for more than 18 months, but my parents were yet to warm to him. It hurt me to see them greeting him with strained smiles, especially when Mum loved to fuss over Faye's Paul, who could do no wrong after proposing to my sister. But Paul was a farm boy from a neighbouring property; to my parents Ian was an outsider who couldn't ride a horse or milk a cow. To make up for this he was extra helpful when repairs were required, and would spend hours walking the hills at the back of the farm to find and shoot vermin like foxes and rabbits, hoping to please Dad. He tried really hard to always be polite, but he could sense their suspicion of him and it made him uncomfortable in their presence, which then meant he often dug himself into a deeper hole as he tried all the harder to please them. He couldn't seem to win a trick.

One weekend at home, Ian produced half a dozen cans of beer. As my parents didn't drink, they weren't happy about that. But for some reason, Ian didn't take any notice of me telling him to put away the beer. He asked my parents, 'Do you mind if I have a drink?' and they said politely, 'No' – the exact opposite of how they really felt, and you could have cut the atmosphere with a knife. In retrospect I put this down to his age and the fact his parents thought social drinking was perfectly acceptable and normal. But of course at the time none of this helped his cause!

Generally I chose to ignore my parents' unspoken undercurrent of disapproval, although there was no doubt I knew what they thought – I'd heard snippets of their opinions from friends. I didn't want endless rows, though, so I bit my tongue and when we were in Cudgewa tried to smooth over any tension as best I could.

Forever hopeful, Ian kept trying to win their approval, continuing to sacrifice some of his Saturday nights with me to go spotlighting on his own. After quietly observing him bringing in an impressive haul of rabbit and kangaroo meat for the farm dogs week after week, one warm summer night Dad finally offered to accompany him up to the paddock. It seemed we'd had something of a breakthrough.

As soon as it was dark, Dad fired up the farm Toyota and after Ian loaded the guns into the back, Ian and I climbed onto the tray at the back. Dad drove the three of us down the meandering farm track and through a gate into the paddock where we could start hunting. As the Toyota trundled slowly across the shrub land, we switched on the spotlight attached to the battery under the bonnet and I was in charge of moving it back and forth as we looked out for roos and rabbits.

'Here, you go first,' Ian said, passing me a single-shot rifle and taking over the spotlight. As he beamed the light on a transfixed kangaroo as tall as a man crouching in the long grass, I lifted the gun to my shoulder and took aim. Releasing the trigger, I sprayed out an ear-splitting burst of bullets, missing the roo and showering empty shells onto the roof of the Toyota.

As I screamed in shock at the unexpected explosion of shot, Ian's mouth twitched with amusement. I knew instantly that he had modified the weapon to make it fire like a machine gun. But while I rolled my eyes and started to laugh despite myself, Dad was livid. 'What the bloody hell do ya think ya doing, wasting all those bullets?' he bellowed. 'If you're gonna muck around, we'll go home.'

The rest of the shoot was carried out in silence and that was the last time Ian used that gun when Dad was around.

Dry-retching behind my surgical mask, I tried hard to breathe through my mouth. In front of me, a surgeon was slicing into an abscess located between the patient's ribs. As a trickle of custard-coloured pus cascaded down the green drapes, the operating theatre was filled with an eggy, rotten odour, leaving Pam and I gagging.

In February 1972 I'd left the wound-care and bed-changing duties of the general wards for an altogether different experience – theatre. Just stepping foot into theatre was a process in itself. The room was cold, bright and clinical, with powerful overhead lights and the heavy scent of hospital grade disinfectant. As a sterile area it was strictly for staff only – and we were forbidden from entering until we'd dressed in scrubs and covered our hair with a paper beret. Only then could we cross the white line of the 'uncontaminated theatre zone' and step into a pair of special boots that were laundered after each use.

In the theatre during an operation there were the scrubbed staff, who handed the surgeon the instruments, and one or two scout nurses, who brought over the equipment the surgeon needed, or removed anything that was in the way. Nothing could leave the room until a final count had been done at the end of the operation to make sure no equipment had been left inside the patient.

Although Pam and I had been instructed to assist during the abscess-removing procedure and had been prepared for the steps involved, we were totally unprepared for the over-powering smells of surgery. Seeing my friend dry-retch set me off laughing behind my mask, and every time I gagged I could see her shoulders shaking too. Heaving intermittently and trying unsuccessfully to compose ourselves, we spent the majority of the surgery with tears streaming down our cheeks. Afterwards, the theatre sister took us aside. 'You can't bugger about like that,' she warned. 'If the surgeon catches you playing up, you'll be for it. Buy some Vicks in your lunchbreak and rub it in your mask.'

It was a valuable lesson learnt, and after that I never went into theatre without an emergency jar of VapoRub in my pocket.

Unexpected smells aside, I loved theatre. It was a unique environment and the doctors and the senior staff were keen to teach anyone who showed an interest in becoming part of that world. To me, every visit was a great learning experience. I would observe intently as the theatre sisters prepared the sterile instruments for each operation and skilled surgeons whipped out tonsils and appendices. As scout nurses, we helped the assisting nurse or sister, and our last task for the day was to thoroughly clean the operating theatre.

Left to our own devices, Pam and I would seize the opportunity to play pranks. One afternoon we dared another student to lie on the operating table. As soon as she'd clambered up, we tied her down with straps and tipped the table to a 30-degree angle. 'Bye!' Pam waved as we abandoned her, swinging out through the doors. Giggling, we huddled out of sight until her indignant cries became a little too loud. We rushed back in and quickly freed her before the commotion alerted a passing sister.

If we hadn't worked together during the day, Pam and I would lounge on each other's beds in the evening, swapping horror stories. 'You wouldn't want to get on the wrong side of the surgeon I've been working with,' she said one night, recounting how he'd screamed at a sister for handing him the wrong forceps and then hurled the instrument back at the trolley.

'I hope I don't get that mongrel,' I said, making a mental note to revise yet again all the different types of instruments.

Typically, exactly one week later, I came face to face with the forcep-thrower, having unwittingly volunteered to be his assisting nurse. Mr James (as he was usually referred to in polite company) would be examining the bowel of a 65-year-old man who'd been suffering acute abdominal pain. I would be passing Mr James any instruments he needed during the procedure and dodging out the way of any he didn't.

Standing beside the surgeon, I watched as he made a 10-centimetre incision into the patient's abdomen. When blood started to ooze from the wound, I handed him a sterile sponge. Next I passed him a kidney dish to place the used scalpel in.

'Get rid of that. I want the twenty-three!' he barked.

With a racing heart I scoured the tray, located the number 23 (a large scalpel blade) and passed it to Mr James in a kidney dish, following the example of other scrub nurses. When no insults or instruments came flying back, I knew I'd got it right. Relaxing a little, I watched as he cut carefully into the patient's abdominal cavity. As he cut into the flesh, it reminded me of Dad butchering a sheep on the farm. Eventually he located the pink, sausage-like bowel.

'This doesn't look good,' he said, holding up a section. It had a purple tinge, which was indicative of bowel cancer.

'Specimen container,' he ordered as he clamped and dissected it. 'That needs to go straight to pathology.'

In the two and a half hours it took to complete the operation, the surgeon barely acknowledged me. Although in hindsight that was probably a good thing (and – I now realise – perfectly normal and good practice!), at the time it did make me wonder if he was furious with the way I'd worked.

But as we removed our boots and left the sterile area, to my surprise John, the male charge sister in theatre, said, 'You handled that very well. You'd make a good theatre sister.'

Changing out of my scrubs, I had mixed feelings. I felt proud, but also sad for the unconscious patient. While his operation had brought positive results for me, he was going to face difficult news when he woke up.

Thankfully not every procedure heralded bad news. On my last day in theatre I saw a doctor remove something a lot less sinister – a newborn baby, by caesarean section.

All eyes were on the obstetrician as he reached into the woman's opened-up abdomen and pulled out a small purple baby attached to a blue, gnarled umbilical cord. I watched, transfixed, as the little fella began to wiggle his arms and legs, and let out a healthy-sounding cry as he was handed to a midwife.

Forgetting the protocol to keep out the way, I stepped forwards to take a closer look. As he squirmed in the midwife's arms, I could see his skin turning pink. I assumed this was due to his first breaths of oxygen but I couldn't be sure. Either way, it was amazing! Noting my interest, the midwife smiled. 'We need to dry him quickly and keep him warm,' she explained as she rubbed the baby with a towel and wrapped him snugly in a hospital blanket. Little did she know she was giving me my first glimpse of my future.

Later that year, I received note in my letterbox at the nurses' home inviting me to the graduation ceremony of the nurses from the year above me. The invitation instructed that I was to wear a starched uniform and clean shoes, and I assumed I'd be set to work as an usherette.

On the allotted day, I arrived in good time at the recreational hall and found Mr Coulson, the tutor sister, in charge. 'What do you want me to do?' I asked him.

'You don't need to do anything, Nurse,' he smiled. 'You're getting an award for surgical nurse of the year.'

'How did I get that?' I asked.

'The charge sister in theatre gave you a glowing report,' he revealed. 'Take a seat at the back and come forward when your name is called.'

Stunned, I took my place next to two other student nurses from my year, who'd known they were getting awards because they'd had the sense to ask when they received the invitation out of the blue. So that weekend I headed home to my parents to proudly show off my prize – a posh black and gold Parker pen with my name engraved on it.

'You'd better leave that with me so you don't lose it,' Dad said with a twinkle in his eye. It was wonderful feeling to make my parents proud, and the award gave me a real boost. It seemed I had chosen the right path.

With the countdown on till Faye and Paul's November wedding, our family discovered we had another reason to celebrate. Faye had been shortlisted for the Miss Victoria Quest after raising $15,000 for a cerebral palsy charity. The gala ball for the competition was to be held in Benalla, Victoria, 117 kilometres from Albury. On the day, Pam, George and I checked into a motel to get ready for the ceremony. Full of anticipation about the night ahead, I had just put on the paisley print dress I was looking forward to showing off and finished my make-up when there was a knock on my door. I was expecting Ian, who was making a special trip up from Puckapunyal for the occasion; instead, I found George.

'Ian's here,' he said. 'But he's drunk.'

Stepping outside, I found Ian struggling to walk straight and stinking of sherry. Worst of all, he seemed to think this was very amusing.

'I don't think you're funny,' I snapped, swatting away his hand as he tried to hold mine. 'You knew tonight was important to me.'

'Can you take him to your room and sober him up?' I pleaded to George. 'Mum and Dad can't see him like this.'

'I'll make him have a shower,' George agreed, manhandling Ian across the car park to his room.

Now for the real challenge – I had to get him through the three-course meal without upsetting my family. I attempted to reduce the risk by seating him out of the direct line of sight of my parents, next to George, who did his best at 'Ian-sitting' and batting away any more alcohol. Throughout the meal I was aware of Ian glancing at me, but I was too angry to reciprocate. Instead I focused on Faye: soon she appeared on stage, looking gorgeous in a gold and black dress with her long hair piled high into a beehive. Sadly she didn't clinch the title, but we all had a good time regardless – even if in my case I achieved that by ignoring Ian. The next morning, as he headed off with Pam and George, I could barely manage a curt goodbye. And I wasn't the only one. 'That fella has no respect for this family,' Dad said, pursing his lips angrily. Apparently Ian's bloodshot eyes hadn't gone unnoticed.

The next time I saw Ian was three weeks later when he arrived in Albury for the Police and Nurses' Ball. Excited about another opportunity to dress up and go dancing, I'd booked us a motel room weeks earlier, but I was still angry about his behaviour in Benalla and it now was a struggle to feel happy about the prospect. When Ian immediately headed for the bar, it only added to my exasperation.

That night I agreed to dance with a good-looking guy I knew from George's football team. After a drink or six, Ian didn't like that one bit and soon we were rowing in the corner. 'You haven't even said sorry for letting me down,' I told him. 'I don't know if I want to be with you anymore.'

Ian didn't drink any more than the rest of his mates and, unlike my parents, I enjoyed an occasional drink as well. But in this case I'd expected an apology and hoped we could talk things through. Instead, Ian refused to stay at the motel, insisting on hitchhiking back to Puckapunyal. After dropping him by the side of the Hume Highway, I drove back to the nurses' home, sobbing.

I tossed and turned that night, and the next morning I felt sick. I had thought I loved Ian and he felt the same, but it was all too hard. His thoughtless behaviour and my parents' disapproval had worn me down. After a couple of evenings of crying in my room, I had to pull myself together. I was only a few months into my third year and I'd have to study hard to make the grade. I had always found exams difficult, and being unattached would make it easier to stay focused on my work. At least that's what I told myself.

Several weeks after our break-up, a junior nurse knocked on my door to tell me I had a visitor. When I got to the lobby I was shocked to find Ian standing there in his army uniform. 'I've been posted back to Bandiana for a month,' he told me. 'Will you come out for tea with me? I just want us to be friends.'

I wasn't sure it was a good idea. But despite still being angry with him, I felt a little guilty about leaving him on the side of the highway, so I agreed. After changing, I found Ian waiting in a flashy white XW Ford Futura.

'I passed my test,' he grinned. He drove us to our old haunt, the Camelot Lounge, where I let him buy me a steak dinner and filled him in on Faye and Paul's wedding the weekend before. I'd had a great time, largely because I'd convinced myself to put Ian out of my mind, determined to enjoy Faye's big day.

The night unfolded in a demure fashion: Ian dropped me at the nurses' home and gave me nothing more than a farewell peck on the cheek. But as I opened the car door he seemed hesitant. He suddenly blurted out, 'Will you come to the movies on Saturday?'

His insistence that he just wanted to be friends didn't last long. The following weekend an arm crept around my shoulder during the movie, and afterwards he asked me to go for coffee. 'I miss you,' he said as we sat in the café. 'What do I have to do to make things up to you?'

'I don't know if you can,' I said with tears in my eyes. 'And I hate upsetting my parents.'

'But you're not going to be with them forever,' he said. 'They don't run your life.'

I knew that, but I loved them and I still liked to please them. It was important to me that they approved of the man I cared enough about to bring home and meet them. By now I was crying.

I didn't relent that day. I couldn't. But Ian was persistent. For the month he was in Bandiana, he constantly turned up at the nurses' home to woo me and his efforts became increasingly hard to resist. By the time he was due to return to his barracks in Puckapunyal, I'd forgiven him and we'd picked up where we left off. Deep down I knew he was the man for me and I loved the way he made me feel. Despite his earlier behaviour, he really was a gentleman, in quite an old-fashioned way – he would buy me dinner, open doors for me and my friends and never swore in front of us. And he was always great fun to be with – I loved his sense of humour. Not only that, but Ian appreciated my own wicked sense of humour, and that I called a spade a spade. He used to compliment me on my deep brown eyes. He said they were not only beautiful but that they reflected my strength of character. And, to cap it all, his mother approved of me!

I look back on us coming together again as a 'sliding door'; I wouldn't be where I am today had I not had Ian by my side so much of the way.

But I had no intention of sharing our reunion with my parents.

Chapter 3
Catching bubs

I gently laid the soapy baby into the shallow bath, and trickled a cupful of water over her chubby tummy. 'To get her used to the sensation,' I said, glancing up at the baby's mother. Bathing a slippery newborn can be nerve-racking, especially if the baby is distressed. However, judging by baby Matilda's peaceful face, she didn't mind the water at all.

After her bath, her mum dressed her, starting with the cloth nappy and pins I'd left within reach of the changing mat. In the 1970s we were all still using cloth nappies, and although nowadays most busy mothers would throw up their hands in horror at the idea, they had lots of advantages, not least that they're more versatile – they can be used as protection against babies' vomit or posseting – less expensive and, of course, far better for the environment.

Working in the nursery wasn't one of my usual rotations and it had been a nice surprise to be asked to cover for a mothercraft nurse who had called in sick that morning. Everyone seemed grateful for my help, but the truth is that it was hardly a chore. Most other wards have a subdued, sober feel to them, but not the nursery. The babies wrapped like parcels in their little metal cots represented the start of life, and the atmosphere was a lively, happy one, with mums chatting as their babes slept in their arms.

I spent the day flitting between baby baths, changes and feeds, and at one point I overheard two women discussing their midwife.

'Did you have Jenny too?' one asked. 'Isn't she amazing? I don't think I could have done it without her.'

I had no idea who Jenny was, but she had clearly been wonderful to these two mothers. Listening to their praise I hoped that one day someone might talk about me like that.

When my shift was over, I checked in with the midwife in charge, Tina. 'You look like you enjoyed today,' she said.

'I did!' I agreed. 'But who wouldn't love working with babies all day?'

'You'd be surprised,' Tina laughed. 'You know, if you enjoy it, you should think about a second certificate in midwifery.'

There were just seven months to go until I graduated as a sister, so the time had come for me to decide what to do next. I could continue to work as a graduate nurse – a first-year qualified nurse who's supported in the role and works in all areas of the hospital – or I could study for a second certificate in order to specialise in a particular field of nursing. I had thought about training to be a theatre sister, but after enjoying my time in the nursery so much I began to seriously consider midwifery as a second certificate, then maternal and child health as a third certificate. I was probably more ambitious than I realised, and doing a triple certificate would give me more opportunities than becoming a theatre sister. I knew that with Ian in the army, midwifery would also be a more flexible option to pursue in line with his different postings around Australia. All things considered, after my experience in the maternity ward, I was convinced that working with babies and mothers-to-be was where I truly belonged.

Still, it was a big decision and I thought I should seek advice before making the final commitment. A long chat on the phone to a midwife friend of Mum's closed the deal for me. 'Midwifery's hard work but rewarding,' she told me. 'If you can stay calm under pressure and you enjoy building a relationship with your patients, it will be perfect for you.'

Once I'd made up my mind, I immediately began to research midwifery schools, focusing on the hospitals nearest to Ian in Puckapunyal. Top of my list was Melbourne's Preston and Northcote Community Hospital (PANCH), where I'd originally wanted to do my nurse training. By this time I had finally confessed to my parents that Ian and I were back together. Although they hadn't protested, I could sense their silent disapproval. But Ian was right, Mum and

Dad didn't run my life and only I could decide what made me happy.

After Christmas and New Year's Eve apart, visiting our families, I was longing to see him. He had spent his army leave 890 kilometres away with his family in Loxton. We reunited in Albury in January 1973, celebrating with dinner and a romantic stroll. As we paused to look out across the water, he held me and kissed me.

'I think we should get married,' he suddenly announced. 'That way we can live together when you've finished your training.'

I laughed. 'I'm serious!' he said. 'I think we should do it. February the twenty-fifth is two years since we met. It's a good date to get engaged.'

It wasn't exactly a traditional proposal but it would do for me! High on the excitement of our decision, we stayed up late into the night making plans. I liked the idea of a spring wedding, when the flowers would be out and there would be less chance of rain. We chose 13th of October – a Saturday in the middle of spring – as our big day.

I was thrilled, but also anxious at the prospect of telling my parents. We spent the next few hours strategically plotting how Ian should ask Dad. I decided that my parents were most relaxed on Saturday evenings, when they liked to retire early to read in bed, so that was the best time to break the news. With our plan in place, I arranged a visit to Cudgewa.

After a tense day of waiting, I beckoned Ian into my parents' room. 'Dad, Ian has something he wants to ask you,'

I said tentatively, perching on the end of their bed, with Ian standing behind me. Peering cautiously over his glasses, Dad put down his newspaper. My mother remained engrossed in her book.

'I'd like to have your permission to marry Beth,' Ian began. He'd barely got the words out when Mum dropped her book and frowned. 'You don't have mine,' she announced in an indignant voice.

'What about you, Dad?' I asked, feeling a bit sick. My father looked pained and sighed deeply. 'Mum's the boss,' he said after a few seconds.

Angry and hurt, I stormed to my bedroom, with Ian trailing behind me, and began to pack up my belongings. I told Ian to do the same. As we headed down the back path of the house to his car, we were intercepted by my pyjama-clad father. 'Where do you think you're going?' he said.

'Back to Albury,' I replied. 'What's the use of Ian staying here when he knows he's not welcome?'

By the time we'd driven down the farm track and out onto the road to Albury, tears were streaming down my face. Why couldn't my parents just be happy for me? Whether Mum and Dad liked it or not, I saw Ian as my soulmate. I couldn't imagine marrying anyone else. I had made my choice.

'Please don't cry,' Ian told me, reaching over to squeeze my hand. 'They can't stop us getting married. We'll do it with or without their blessing.'

In contrast to my family, Ian's parents were thrilled with the news: they were glad he'd found a 'nice nurse' to keep him on the straight and narrow. 'You don't have to worry about a thing,' Ian's mum soothed as we told her about my parents' reaction. 'Angus and I will pay for the wedding if necessary.'

Three weeks after we had left my parents' place with such bad feeling, Mum called the nurses' home. 'How are you?' she asked tentatively.

'I'm busy planning the wedding,' I told her coldly. 'Ian and I are announcing our engagement in the paper this Saturday.'

I braced myself for a tongue-lashing, but instead Mum paused. 'I wanted to let you know that I hope Ian can make you happy,' she said softly. It was the last thing I'd expected her to say.

'Thanks,' I croaked, suddenly finding it difficult to talk.

'When are your next days off?' she said. 'You'd better come home so we can start making plans.'

After arranging to visit them that weekend, I hung up with tears in my eyes. Having my parents' support, even reluctantly, was a huge weight off my mind.

Now that we were engaged, it seemed silly to make Ian spend nights in Albury cramped in his car – especially when my new ground-floor room was so easy to sneak into. On the nights I planned to break the rules, we'd meet in the lobby, talking in whispers until I'd ascertained the coast was clear. Ian would quickly remove his boots and tiptoe along the corridor to my room.

We had our fair share of close calls. One night I gave Ian the green light to head across the hall to use the toilet. As he relieved himself in a cubicle, he was alarmed to hear a nurse enter the next stall. It took her ages to get on with things, with Ian caged like a trapped animal right next to her.

'I was terrified she'd spot my hairy legs under the door,' he said when he eventually escaped back to my room.

Another morning I'd just let him out of the front door when he found himself cornered by two nurses, walking towards the entrance from either direction. 'Good morning, girls!' he announced cheerily, hoping they hadn't noticed his lack of footwear or the boots he was suspiciously hiding behind his back. Thankfully they seemed oblivious and Ian was able to hot-foot it to his car.

For the next four months I was absorbed with planning the wedding and studying hard to pass my exams. I got an interview at PANCH and to my great relief and pleasure was offered a place to start my midwifery training in December. Everything was falling into place.

My last day at Albury Base Hospital was 14 July 1973. It might have been a sad day had it not been for my colleagues. First they stuck a sign on my dress that said 'BIG BOOB BETH'; next they conspired to give me a cold bath. When I managed to dodge that, they smothered me in baby powder.

'I won't miss you at all!' I lied.

Saying goodbye to Pam proved to be the hardest moment. Watching her and George carrying boxes of her belongings out of the nurses' home, I had a lump in my throat. For three years we'd been partners in crime, swapping stories, gossiping about boyfriends and falling into fits of laughter at inappropriate moments. It was the end of an era. In three weeks she would marry George and start work as a general nurse at Corowa Hospital.

'Don't look so sad, I'll see you at the wedding!' she said, grabbing me in a tight bear hug. 'Good luck at Corryong!'

Now I was a qualified nurse, I had a temporary job lined up working the night shift at Corryong Hospital, where Faye worked. It would give me the opportunity to live rent-free with Mum and Dad before the wedding and our move to Melbourne. When they weren't dealing with bus-crash emergencies, Corryong kept fewer than 15 patients in over-night. Faye said that night shifts were usually quiet and the majority of my time would be spent holding the fort at the nurses' desk or helping the odd patient to the toilet. It seemed like a good place to break myself in as a sister.

Not long after I'd started at Corryong, late one quiet August night, the shrill ring of the ward telephone made me jump. It was Judy, a double-certificate midwife, asking me to help her in the labour room. When I got there I found a rotund young woman lying naked on her back on the bed. She was panting and groaning, in the depths of labour. Judy stood next to her dressed in a white gown and surgical mask.

'You need to ring the doctor,' she said. 'Rosie is ready for delivery.'

The duty doctor (a GP, since this was a country hospital) answered quickly when I called him at home, and I nerv-ously passed on Judy's message. 'Is she fully dilated?' he asked me. I was four months away from beginning my midwifery training, and I had no idea what *that* meant.

'She's ready for delivery,' I repeated. 'Judy said you need to come.'

Back in the delivery room, Judy seemed fraught. 'Help me,' she said. 'Get a gown and mask on. We need to get Rosie into stirrups.'

After covering my uniform in a clean white gown, I helped Judy attach the leg holders to the bed and we wrestled Rosie's writhing legs into the padded supports and wrapped the tapes around her ankles. I had seen these poles used in theatre during my training for some gynaecological procedures, but in those cases the women would be under anaesthetic. This woman was in labour and it looked to me like she needed to be able to move. It seemed so barbaric! Then Judy released the end of the bed, tucking it under the top half, and placed a metal bucket on the floor.

Rosie was sobbing. 'I want to go home!' she suddenly screeched, glaring at her husband. 'I can't stand this.' The poor man looked downright terrified and bewildered but he rallied and came forward to try to comfort his wife.

'She's very close,' Judy confirmed quietly to me. 'Keep her cool, give her plenty of water and help lift her head when she starts pushing.'

I mopped Rosie's forehead with a damp cloth. 'The doctor's on his way,' I told her as I offered her water. I had no idea what else to say. Either way, Rosie didn't appear to be listening. As she began to thrash and sob through another contraction, I felt my heart pounding in my chest. Was this normal? How much pain could one person take?

My panicked thoughts were interrupted by the arrival of a stern-looking man in his late fifties. 'Why did you call me?' he demanded, eyes darting between Judy and me.

'Rosie is fully dilated,' Judy replied. 'The baby will be here any moment now.'

Barely grunting an acknowledgement, the doctor began to scrub up, surveying the scene sternly. Slipping his fingers into sterile rubber gloves, he stood with his arms folded, waiting. As Rosie began to push, grimacing and grunting, I gently supported her head. I could see the veins in her neck bulging as she strained, yet after 20 minutes of this agonising effort, there was still no baby in sight.

'Pass me a syringe and local anaesthesic,' the doctor demanded. He injected Rosie in the soft skin behind her vagina. I watched, horrified, as he picked up a pair of scissors and cut her from the vagina towards the anus. Suddenly, the baby's head appeared to explode out from within.

Of all the things I had imagined about childbirth, it was not that it would resemble a ghastly scene from a slasher film. Within seconds the body had emerged, the baby slipping into the doctor's hands with a gush of bloody amniotic fluid. As it streamed down the bed drapes, I suddenly understood the purpose of the bucket. Taking the rather dazed baby, Judy cleaned him up and handed him to his mother. I smiled as Rosie cradled him, gasping with choked sobs of joy. Magically, all the pain and fear seemed to have been forgotten in this tender moment.

I noticed that the doctor seemed preoccupied as he studied the severed umbilical cord protruding from between Rosie's legs. Just when I thought I'd seen it all, he held the cord tautly. Moving his hand slowly, he started to pull until a grey, slippery organ that looked like lamb's liver plopped out. Holding it up like a prize catch, he dropped it into a kidney dish.

'That's the placenta,' Judy whispered, amused by my stunned expression. Clearly I had a lot to learn.

After the doctor had stitched up the nasty wound in Rosie's bottom, Judy transferred mother and baby to maternity, leaving me to clean up. Collecting the blood-soaked drapes and towels, I was still reeling at how brutal and gory childbirth seemed to be. The caesarean birth I'd witnessed as a student had seemed so sedate and controlled in comparison.

'Still want to be a midwife, Beth?' Judy asked with a wry smile when she returned to the room.

'I think so,' I nodded, not altogether convinced. Well, it was too late to change my mind now.

We got married just after my 21st birthday. Our wish for a perfect spring day was granted: I woke on 13 October to blue skies and a beautiful mild temperature. Stepping into the wedding car in my white 'baby doll' dress, I clutched my trail bouquet of stephanotis and lily-of-the-valley. The butterflies in my stomach were soothed by Dad, who climbed in next to me to take my hand. 'I hope this is going to be a wonderful day for you,' he said. 'Mum and I hope you're making the right decision.'

At St John's Anglican Church in Wodonga, I was met by my bridesmaids: Pam, who was now a married woman herself, my sister Faye, and Barbara, my best friend from high school. As they began to help me out the car we were intercepted by my brother-in-law, Paul. 'Don't get out,' he panted. 'Ian's parents aren't here yet!'

I never did tell my in-laws that I had watched, amused, from the car as they sprinted up the church path and quickly took their place alongside Ian's sister, Jenny. With everyone finally assembled, I walked up the aisle with Dad to join Ian for a short, heartfelt service. At the end of it I felt so blissfully happy, and bathed in a sense of quiet achievement; Ian and I were married at last and I'd managed to overcome my parents' expectations. Most importantly, I knew I'd made the right decision.

We held our reception at the New Albury Hotel, where Dad delivered his father-of-the-bride speech with genuine warmth and no hint of his struggle to accept Ian. Then we packed up the car and hit the road as man and wife. It was time to start our new life.

✳

While we hunted for a flat in Melbourne, we stayed with Ian's aunt and uncle. As my midwifery training wasn't scheduled to begin for another two months, I was grateful that PANCH had given me a general nursing job. However, my first assignment was the Intensive Care Unit, and the last place I wanted to be as an inexperienced graduate nurse was in the ICU of a bustling city hospital. On my first day, as I surveyed the beds of comatose patients, lying deathly still with wires attached to their chests and limbs, I felt my stomach knot with nerves. I'd never cared for such seriously ill people or seen so many machines.

After a hasty introduction my mentor, Jane, ushered me over to a young, seemingly lifeless man on a ventilator.

'Motorbike accident,' she said. 'He needs a sponge bath then we'll lift and move him to relieve the pressure on his skin.'

As Jane ran me through the functions of the heart and blood pressure monitors, we were interrupted by a blast of bells. I'd heard about 'Code Blues', when a patient is in immediate need of life-saving resuscitation, but this was the first time I'd experienced one. Jane reacted immediately and I chased her down the ward and watched, my heart in my mouth, as she darted to the side of a woozy-looking middle-aged man and released a lever to knock his bed flat. As the patient's head lolled to one side, a doctor ran forward and started cardiac compressions. I stood at a safe distance, feeling helpless as my new colleagues brought him back from the brink.

'I had no idea what was happening,' I confided to Ian that evening. 'I'm completely out of my depth.'

After a week learning the ropes, however, I began to feel more confident. It helped that because I was only a graduate nurse, there was always someone more qualified working alongside me whom I could consult.

Although I went about my duties with a smile, my emotions always ran high in the ICU. Some days there were good outcomes, with patients making formidable recoveries, but some days there were no happy endings. It was hard to take day after day and I found it gruelling being in the thick of this acute area of the hospital.

One of my saddest moments was looking after a 66-year-old man who had suffered a stroke. Initially he was conscious, which gave his wife and daughter hope; however, when his brain began to swell there was nothing more the doctors could do. He was brain dead before the end of the day. His family surrounded the bed and said their goodbyes. It was impossible to walk away unaffected from these tragic moments. A life lost in an instant.

After eight weeks, I left the ICU with a great sense of relief and a lifelong respect for the staff who worked there. It takes enormous skill to know what immediate action is required to save a life, and great strength of character and professionalism to carry on when the outcome so often is not a good one.

*

Finally, after a three-month delay and a stint on a general surgical ward, I began my midwifery training in March 1974.

I was at last starting out on my chosen career and even at this early stage, I had a strong sense that this was a calling rather than simply a job.

Early in the afternoon of my sixth day, an alert came over the speaker: 'Student midwives to Delivery'. Rushing through the double swinging doors of the maternity unit, I grabbed a gown, theatre hat and mask. Immediately I was swept up in a rush of orange-frocked fledgling midwives dropping whatever they were doing to race to the birth suite for an all-important 'witness'. As a student I had to witness 10 births before I'd be allowed to deliver a baby myself.

'*Just watch*,' my teacher, Heather, whispered as she held the door open and ushered me into the room. 'We'll talk about the birth afterwards.'

Shuffling in quietly behind another student, I stood with my back against the wall and tried to be as inconspicuous as possible – not exactly easy in a 5-square-metre room. A dark-haired woman in a white hospital gown lay on the delivery bed with her legs strapped in stirrups. As she gripped on to the polls of the stirrups, trying to push out her baby, each panting effort pulled her nearer to the end of the bed. When her contraction subsided, the doctor and midwife helped her back again.

From the few words the woman and her husband had spoken since I'd been in the room, I could tell she was a Greek immigrant. In those days, PANCH didn't have interpreters and I doubted anyone had asked her permission before inviting half the hospital to watch her give birth. With a couple of stragglers behind me there were six students, our teacher, Heather, a doctor and two other midwives. It felt intrusive.

Pushing the thought from my mind, I stood with my eyes fixed on the small black dot of the baby's head, which was growing ever bigger between the woman's quivering thighs. Then I spotted an array of sharp tools on a tray next to the doctor and I wondered with a jolt if he would cut her, as had happened during the last, terrifying birth I'd seen. But instead he stayed still, as we all did, watching and waiting. Meanwhile, the baby's head kept coming, stretching the woman's vagina to what looked to me like an eye-watering diameter.

I watched, amazed, as a downy scalp emerged, followed by two tiny eyebrows, then, slowly but surely, the mucus-covered eyes, nose and lips. As the doctor sprang into action, cupping the baby's head with his hands, a midwife used a suction tube to clear the baby's mouth and nose. The anticipation in the room was palpable as we waited for the all-important catch. The baby arrived beautifully, sliding effortlessly into the doctor's outstretched hands. It was a little boy, plump and olive-skinned like his father, but wearing the disgruntled frown of an old man. With the placenta swiftly delivered and the baby boy left to nestle in his mother's arms, Heather ushered us from the room. Glancing back I caught the mother's eye.

'*Thank you*,' I mouthed.

Chapter 4
Chasing the deliveries

After six weeks on the public postnatal ward at PANCH, I was to rotate on to the labour ward, or the delivery suite as it was sometimes called. In those days, we never used the word 'birthing'. We delivered babies, and all labouring women went to the delivery suite. It's only in the past 15 years that the terminology has changed, the rationale being 'Midwives assist women to birth babies. Pizza boys do deliveries.'

When I first started in the delivery suite, I felt like I had returned to theatre – we had to dress in theatre scrubs, and scrub and wear sterile gloves for procedures such as vaginal examinations and deliveries. The difference was the women were awake! I loved the way the midwives encouraged and pampered the women in labour, along with the way everyone made me feel welcome as a novice student. By now I'd witnessed a number of births, and couldn't wait to start trying my hand at assisting them.

When labouring women were brought in, it was my job to give them their initial assessment. As they lay on the bed, I checked their temperature, pulse and blood pressure and timed their contractions. Next, I'd feel for the position and presentation of the baby and listen to the foetal heart. Once my notes had been double-checked by a senior midwife, I'd carry out the two tasks I hated the most, and my patients no doubt hated even more – the full pubic and perineal shave and enema.

Our tutors insisted these procedures were necessary to reduce the risk of infection to the baby during birth, but I nevertheless did them reluctantly, and couldn't help but think that there must be a better way. Surely the last thing a woman in labour wanted was an intimate shave and a tube of fluid squeezed up her backside? And although the women rarely complained, I hated seeing their discomfort. There is nothing pleasant about shaving someone already in pain, then sending her waddling to the toilet.

Thankfully, by the late 1970s hospitals began to recognise that a woman in labour does not need an enema as her body will empty the bowel naturally to make way for the baby, and it was eventually accepted that hair does not create an infection risk, so nor do labouring women need to be shaved. These days many mothers-to-be arrive with Brazilian waxes, but that's their choice, not one forced upon them in the throes of labour.

It was a big day when I finally got the chance to catch my first baby in the birth suite. Until then, my 'catches' had been limited to plastic babies delivered through wooden pelvises, but with the help of my mentor, Julie, I was at last going to deliver a real live baby. As a midwife, your first 'catch' is something you never forget, and it was no different for me.

I had been caring for a second-time mother, Tracy, ever since I'd come on duty at 2.30 pm. She knew I was a student and had been very accommodating. Now, with my hand laid gently on her abdomen, I sat spellbound, feeling her uterus tighten and relax.

'Have you noticed how the sensation changes as Tracy gets nearer to giving birth?' Julie asked. 'Watching and waiting and feeling subtle changes like this is the best way to follow the progress of labour.'

I nodded. I had been tracking Tracy's temperature and blood pressure and the wellbeing of the baby, using my pinard, a small trumpet-like stethoscope, to listen to its heart rate. Having clocked up 10 'witnesses' while working on the postnatal ward, I was now well accustomed to the procedures, sounds and intensity of birth. Even the episi-otomies, which happened frequently in those days, didn't seem as gruesome as the one I'd seen at Corryong before I had any experience of birth. My biggest fear about delivering a baby at this point was that I would drop it in the bucket.

'Give Tracy some space now,' Julie instructed, as my patient began to suffer through a wave of pain. 'No woman wants to be prodded during a contraction.'

As Tracy's husband let out a cry of pain and tried to remove his hand from his wife's crushing grip, Julie glanced at me knowingly. 'She's getting close,' she confirmed. 'Start setting up the delivery trolley. I'll call for Kerry.'

Taking care not to contaminate any of the instruments, I lined up a collection of sterile scissors, forceps and kidney dishes on the trolley and began to scrub up, thoroughly washing from the tips of my fingers to my elbows. Kerry, another senior midwife, arrived to help Julie put Tracy's legs into stirrups. By the end of my midwifery training in 1975, the practice of using stirrups during deliveries had become more relaxed for a normal birth, just as the routine shaves and enemas were beginning to be questioned. Women had started to object, and as a profession we had to sit up and take notice of them, although some dyed-in-the-wool older obstetricians refused to change their ways. The stirrups remained, however, during any assisted delivery, such as with a vacuum or forceps, and that is still the case even today.

Kerry offered Tracy some water, and Julie took her place next to me. An obstetric doctor also joined us. He stood at the back, ready to assist if called upon. The procedure for public patients in most big hospitals in those days was to be sure the on-duty obstetrician – usually a resident – was ready to assist us. A private patient's obstetrician would be expected to personally deliver the baby. When a birth went smoothly, most of the time we would have preferred to have got on with it on our own. But if anything went awry, it was a relief to have the doctor on hand to help out or take over.

'I don't think it'll be long now, Tracy,' said Julie. 'Do you feel ready to push?'

Letting out a long groan, Tracy called out, 'It's coming, it's coming!'

Julie motioned for me to look between her legs. 'Well done!' she encouraged. 'We can see the baby's head!'

Tracy battled on, her body allowing her the briefest of respites before forcing her back into action. She groaned with the effort until, finally, her baby's bald scalp began to crown. Julie grabbed my left hand and placed it on top of the head. 'Keep the head flexed,' she instructed quietly. 'Now use your right hand to place one of those gauze squares over the anal area. Don't take your hand off the head.'

Julie meant me to apply gentle pressure to the emerging baby's head to control the push from 'popping' out of the vagina and thus avoid any major tearing of the perineum – the piece of skin between the vagina and the anus.

Looking up, she raised her voice for Tracy to hear. 'One more push, darling,' she called out cheerfully. 'Okay, now pant, pant, pant; just breathe your baby out.'

Julie guided my hands – one to the top of the emerging head and the other to cover the anal area with the surgical sponge. Once the baby's head was out, we had to use a suction tube to aspirate the mouth then nose so the baby wouldn't inhale mucus with its first breath. Everything was suddenly happening so fast and I was so intensely focused on the juggling act I had to perform that it almost overrode my fear of doing something wrong.

Julie now instructed me to cup my hands over the baby's ears. Then she helped me to rotate the baby's head, to assist with delivering the shoulders. My heart was racing with anticipation. All of a sudden, I had a baby in my hands. A girl! She was wet and slimy and starting to squirm. She gave a husky cry as I held her close, terrified about altering my grip while Julie clamped the cord.

'Here, let me take her,' Kerry smiled, quickly giving her a once-over before she handed her to Tracy, who was looking to her husband. He had tears in his eyes. As the baby was handed to Tracy, he bent and kissed his wife and then placed his lips on the forehead of his new baby daughter.

'I'm so proud of you both,' he said, choking back his emotions. Tracy looked both exhausted and ecstatic. She couldn't take her eyes off her little girl.

But there was no time for us to stop and coo. We still had work to do. 'Third stage now, Beth,' Julie said, placing my left hand on Tracy's abdomen. 'Does it feel like a cricket ball? That's the uterus contracting to expel the placenta.'

With Julie guiding me, I used my other hand to gently pull the umbilical cord. Suddenly I could feel the placenta coming away from within Tracy's uterus. It slid out surprisingly easily, with a trail of membrane and fresh blood, and tumbled into a kidney dish I had placed under Tracy's bottom. Pleased to see that Tracy had no more than a small graze on the skin behind her vagina, I released her legs from the stirrups.

'Well done, Beth,' Julie said. 'That was a textbook birth.'

I was thrilled, relieved and eager to take a look at young Ava, as Tracy had already named her.

'Thanks, Beth,' Tracy said, glancing up to smile appreciatively.

'Don't thank me,' I laughed. 'You're the one who did all the work!'

Secretly, though, I was bursting with pride. It had taken several years and a lot of study and hard slog to get to this point, and learning the mechanisms of labour had been a challenge, but with this first, wonderful birth, I felt the penny was dropping and I was beginning to put together everything I'd learnt. And Ava was the result.

To me, this little baby seemed like a miracle!

In order to qualify as a midwife I needed to complete 20 normal births in my five rotations in the delivery suite. During the 12 months I was also required to work in the antenatal ward, the postnatal ward and the special care nursery, all in six-week rotations. Just over half of our training was in the delivery suite, including two lots of night duty. As the pressure grew to increase my birth tally, I was grateful that I'd had Julie looking out for me when the time had come to catch my first baby. Knowing she had confidence in me helped me to have confidence in myself.

It was also Julie who helped me to master the art of palpation, which means examining someone using one's sense of touch. She always encouraged me to feel and measure women in her care until I could successfully identify the lie of the baby.

A birth didn't count on my record unless I'd attended to the end, which meant delivering the placenta as well. One day, as I oversaw this third stage of labour, pulling gently on the mother's umbilical cord I was alarmed to feel a sensation that didn't seem quite right.

'I think I felt it tear,' I whispered to Julie.

'Just leave it for a couple of minutes then start again,' she said.

Once I felt that the mother's uterus was still contracted like a cricket ball, I reapplied gentle pressure to her belly and I pulled the cord. Almost immediately it severed and sprang away – minus the placenta. Horrified, I turned to Julie.

'Don't panic,' she said. 'It still might come on its own. We need to wait a little longer.'

Although she seemed calm, I felt far from reassured. When the placenta fails to detach, or partially separates from the uterus, the uterus can't contract properly, and this can lead to severe blood loss, or a post-partum haemorrhage (PPH), as it is usually called. What if my patient started bleeding?

Twenty minutes later there was no sign of the placenta delivering spontaneously, and I had the unenviable task of informing my patient she would now need surgery.

Thankfully, it took no time for arrangements to be made to transfer her to theatre so the obstetrician could remove the placenta under a general anaesthetic. This worked out fine, but that didn't stop me feeling awful, and embarrassed. It definitely galvanised me to hone my technique. With experience I learnt to identify by feel the sensation that alerts you to when the cord is about to tear, and to stop pulling.

At some point in their career, a midwife will have to deal with a post-partum haemorrhage, and as it turned out it wasn't long after this that I experienced my first. I was on night duty and in the early hours I answered the bedside bell of a first-time mum, Alice, who had come from the delivery suite earlier that evening.

'I think I'm bleeding,' she told me.

Pulling back the blankets, I switched on my torch and shone the beam down the bed. There was a pool of blood oozing from between Alice's legs. I rang the bell three times to alert my colleagues, but when I peered down the ward there was no sign of anyone. I realised with dismay they must still be feeding the babies in the nursery.

'I'll be back in one minute,' I said to Alice. 'I just need to get something.'

The nursery was a good 20-metre walk from the ward and as soon as I was out of Alice's sight I began to run.

'You need to come quick,' I panted as I burst in there, startling Julie, the senior midwife on duty that night. 'I have a woman bleeding and I need help. Can you phone the registrar then come to room 6 while I go back to her?'

I ran back to Alice and wedged cotton pads between her legs. By now the sheets were drenched and the blood was pooling at an alarming rate. I knew I was dealing with a post-partum haemorrhage.

'What's happening?' Alice asked with panic in her voice. 'I feel sick.'

When Julie arrived she began to rub Alice's abdomen, trying to stimulate the uterus to contract, which would help to stop the bleeding. The doctor had been called and I'd fetched the ergometrine – medication that would hopefully help to force Alice's uterus to contract.

We gave Alice the medicine and Julie asked me to take over kneading Alice's stomach. Despite my best efforts I could feel her uterus relaxing rather than showing signs of contracting under my hand.

'Stop it, it hurts!' Alice cried out, trying to push my hand away. Now sweaty and woozy from the blood loss, she looked dangerously close to passing out. Another huge clot oozed between her legs and I felt very frightened for her. My heart was pounding in my chest but I tried to keep calm and focus on following Julie's instructions.

'We've got a PPH,' Julie called out, spotting the resident doctor at the top of the ward. 'We need to get this girl to theatre now.'

Quickly setting Alice up with a drip, we pulled the bed away from the wall and wheeled her to theatre. With her fate now in the hands of PANCH's skilled obstetricians, there was nothing more we could do.

Back in the ward I had my work cut out calming some other mothers who had been awoken by the commotion and were understandably concerned. Once the lights were out again and everyone was settled, I joined my colleagues back at the nurses' desk. My hands were still shaking and my mind was racing as I replayed what had unfolded. Had I helped Alice quickly enough? Would she be okay?

When the phone rang 45 minutes later, I braced myself for bad news, but as Julie replaced the receiver she looked relieved. 'Alice is out of surgery now,' she said. 'They found a small piece of placenta, and they've removed it. She lost a lot of blood so they've given her a transfusion. Well done, Beth, for acting so quickly.'

My hands still shaking, I let out a sigh of relief.

My rotations on the night shift were not, however, usually this fraught. Mostly they entailed manning the fort from the nurses' desk and answering the call of any mums who needed help with pain or a trip to the toilet.

Two o'clock in the morning was feeding time for the babies in the nursery and by far our busiest time. When all the cots were filled it took quite a bit of work to help the on-duty mothercraft nurse get the babies suckling on their overnight feed. It seems unbelievable now, but at PANCH in 1974, at night the babies were given boiled water rather than milk. The prevailing wisdom – which as a 22-year-old rookie I didn't think to question – was that in order to be taught to sleep through the night, a baby should not become accustomed to feeding from the mother's breast, or from a bottle of milk; instead, he or she should be given a small amount of water. Ideally the baby would then go back to sleep as quickly as possible. Unsurprisingly, since boiled water does not have the hunger-relieving or sleep-inducing effects of breastmilk, most would struggle to resettle. Often there would be a dreadful racket when they woke and bawled for a feed.

Although such practices were entirely the norm then, when I heard stories of midwives passing from cot to cot propping up babies' bottles with nappies in order to allow infants to feed themselves, it struck me as a terribly dangerous thing to do. What if a baby choked?

To deal with our tiny army of insomniacs, a member of staff would sometimes sneak down to the kitchen and grab sachets of honey, which was smeared on to the babies' dummies so that they would suckle and fall asleep. A twenty-first century mum might find the idea of these kinds of settling techniques unbelievable, but they really did happen, and of course they really did work – although I would certainly strongly recommend against them now that we are more enlightened about dental hygiene and the kinds of foods tiny babies should ingest!

When there weren't many babies in the nursery, I would spend a lot of the night reading or chatting to my colleagues to stay awake. One quiet night I was sitting at the desk talking to a senior midwife when she realised she'd forgotten to make anything for her daughter's preschool fete the following day.

'We could make toffee in the food room?' I suggested, recalling how I had made lollies as a teenager. 'All we need is sugar and water and a few drops of vinegar. We can use the nipple bowls to set the toffee!'

Nipple bowls, small stainless steel dishes, were more usually filled with sterile water and given to mothers so they could wash their nipples before putting the baby to the breast. But my colleague seemed to like this idea, so I headed down to the kitchen to find sachets of sugar and vinegar. For the next hour we had a wonderful time boiling up toffee in the food room, before carefully tidying up and sterilising all the equipment. My colleague finished her shift with a pile of toffee for her daughter's fete but I'm sure she didn't mention to anyone buying it that it had been rustled up in hospital nipple bowls.

In the maternity wing at PANCH, it was usual for new mothers to stay with us between five and seven days while they learnt to care for their babies. As a student midwife I was tasked with helping to bathe and change the newborns. I also stripped the beds and emptied the dirty linen skips, which inevitably smelt a bit ripe. Then, at four-hourly intervals, I'd oversee the breastfeeding – again following a regimented routine.

First, the mothers were ordered to wash their nipples with sterile cottonwool and water. Then, once their babies had latched on, we'd have to time the proceedings. The rule was that a new mother should feed her baby for just three minutes on each breast. Although the amount of time on the nipple extended daily, it seemed unkind to pull a hungry baby away from his mother's breast. But those were the rules and we had to follow them.

'If the baby's still hungry, give it cool, boiled water,' I was told by Gayle, the strict charge sister. Her explanation was that limited feeding prevented the mothers from developing sore nipples. However, I suspected it was more about lessening the workload for the staff. If a mother developed cracked nipples, she or a midwife would need to express the milk from her breasts, a time-consuming, uncomfortable and labour-intensive procedure no one enjoyed.

Gayle was also a stickler for 'compulsory nursery time', enforced between the hours of 12.30 and 2 pm and then from 10.30 pm until the early morning feed at 6 am. When the babies were in the nursery, their mothers were supposed to be resting. This was easier to enforce during the night than the daytime, when it was not unusual to find an anxious mum pacing the corridor, adamant she could hear her baby crying.

'That's not your baby,' a poker-faced Gayle would scold, before dispatching her back to bed. Yet the majority of the time it really was. All baby wails may sound the same to midwives, but somehow a mother just knows her baby's cry; maternal primal instinct is extraordinary.

When I wasn't on the postnatal wards, I continued to observe births and catch babies, and could now add complicated deliveries to my list of experiences. The most common of these were breech and multiple births, and both were potentially life-threatening for the baby and the mother.

In those days, it was not uncommon for breech babies to be delivered vaginally. I will never forget the first one I witnessed. As the baby began to make his entrance, backside first, a plump leg dangled out and the obstetrician explained, 'At this point we keep our hands off the breech.' A second leg flopped out, and as the baby's torso made good progress, the baby's arms were carefully freed. Then the obstetrician coolly stretched out his right forearm. Using it to support the baby, he hooked his index finger into the little boy's mouth, a manoeuvre I'd been taught would keep the head flexed, aiding the delivery. Then, placing his left hand at the nape of the neck, he pulled slowly, as he freed the little fellow's face from the birth canal.

I was surprised at how simple this backwards birth had seemed and would have jumped at the chance to assist with one. However, breech babies at PANCH were always delivered by an obstetrician, and mostly without difficulty. I suppose things changed because having a 'mostly' good outcome will never make up for the tragedy of a baby's life being lost during a breech birth. When things did go wrong, they often went spectacularly wrong. During a breech birth, the baby's head could be too slow to deliver, and entrapment of the head and the consequent lack of oxygen (hypoxia) meant the infant almost certainly wouldn't survive. So as maternity wings became increasingly well set up for and adept at carrying out caesarean sections, this became the preferred, risk-free way to deliver these babies. It also avoided the risk of litigation against the attending staff.

When I started at PANCH in the 1970s we didn't have the benefit of ultrasounds, which nowadays give midwives and mothers such an amazing view inside the womb. Ultrasound was just starting to be used in obstetrics in the late 1970s, but it wasn't until the mid to late 1980s that it was used by most private obstetricians. So in those days it was not unusual to be blindsided by a surprise multiple birth, the most common of which was, of course, twins.

Back then, after the birth, it was routine to palpate the stomach to check there wasn't another baby in there. Only then could you administer an injection of oxytocin, which was used to help detach the placenta.

One day I had just handed a healthy but small baby girl to her smiling mother when I noticed Donna, my supervising midwife that day, looking perplexed. 'We're not done yet,' she said as she ran her hands over the woman's abdomen. 'There's another one in here.'

Sure enough, 30 minutes later, I introduced a second diminutive daughter to her shocked parents. 'Well, I hope that's the last one,' the father announced dryly.

This was the second time I had seen a set of undiagnosed twins born, and both times the levels of anxiety in the room escalated. There's good reason to be concerned when you realise another, and unexpected, baby is on its way, because the statistics show the second (or third!) baby has more risk of complications during the birth. (As with breech births, nowadays most obstetricians prefer to deliver twins or any multiple birth by caesarean section as it is seen to reduce poor outcomes for the mother and her babies.)

In this case, a paediatrician and an obstetrician had been called and an extra baby resuscitation trolley wheeled in, in case there were complications and we needed to carry out a vacuum or forceps birth. Luckily none of the specialised equipment was needed, and the second baby made its entrance into the world with a very loud and healthy cry. All was well.

Now Mum and Dad knew Ian was going to be around for a while, they realised they had to try to overcome their reservations about him and learn to accept him. Ian and I managed to get a few days off over Christmas and we drove to Cudgewa to spend it with them and try to build some bridges. When we arrived, my father was in a black mood because a local mechanic had made a shoddy job of fixing the tank on the back of his Toyota. Dad needed the tank in good working order so he could spray thistles and briars with weedkiller as he drove around the farm, but the spray pump on the tank wasn't working properly.

'Would you like me to have a look at it?' Ian asked.

'You could try,' Dad shrugged. 'But the bloody thing's buggered if you ask me.'

Pulling on their boots they headed off to have a look, and when they returned to the house an hour later, Dad seemed pleased. I watched, amazed, as he opened the fridge and handed Ian one of the lesser-spotted beers that only made it into the house at Christmas time. I could only assume the spray pump was now working like a charm, thanks to Ian.

'See, Dad, if Ian can't fix it, you need to throw it out,' I laughed, and was pleased to see my father nodding in agreement.

From that time on Dad would always have a list of repairs for Ian when we visited Cudgewa, and Mum and Dad's frosty relationship with him slowly began to thaw.

Towards the end of my student year, at the beginning of 1975, I was still trying to get my numbers. I had completed five complicated births, finished my special care nursery case studies, so now I just needed to get my 'catches' at normal births up to 20. Sometimes I'd spend my entire shift looking after a woman, only for her doctor to appear at the last minute to take over the delivery. If a patient had private insurance, this was just the way it was. Yet I often found myself hoping a doctor would be late so I would get the catch instead.

One day I stood, hands poised, when the obstetrician walked in. 'Oh, wonderful,' he said, washing his hands and arms in the sink. 'Thanks, sis, I'll take over now.'

I was bitterly disappointed. I had been so close. Once more, I had built a great rapport with the woman and her husband, only to be cast aside now. 'Don't worry, you got the best part,' Julie said later, attempting to appease me. 'There'll be others.'

74

I appreciated her words, but I couldn't help feeling miffed. While some doctors had a great bedside manner, I often wondered why others were so keen to take charge at the crucial moment. Nothing irritated me more than hearing a GP urging, 'Push! Push! Push!' in an impatient tone, because, I knew, he wanted to get back to a waiting room overflowing with patients. Yet there I was, with all the time in the world to do this job. Would it really be so outrageous to just let me finish the delivery? After all, I was trained to do this.

Despite my frustrations, eventually I got my 20th delivery. I'd had a busy morning restocking and cleaning one of the birthing rooms when I was called.

'Start to set up, Beth,' Julie instructed after introducing me to Belinda, a second time-mother. 'We won't have to wait long for this baby.'

Soon Belinda was growling through gritted teeth that she wanted to push. 'Quick. Scrub before the next contraction,' Julie ordered. I pulled on my gown and rubber gloves just as Belinda's contractions rolled into full force. In no time at all her baby's head was in my hands.

'That's the worst of it!' I told her. 'Now push again when you get the urge and your baby will be here.'

As I cradled the little screeching boy, I looked at Julie triumphantly. There would be no more counting.

✳

I loved working at PANCH and would have been happy to continue my career there, but for 18 months Ian had been

75

making a gruelling 200-kilometre round trip to work, so I'd promised to find a job nearer to his army base in Puck-apunyal. There was no army housing available for us in Puckapunyal or in the neighbouring town of Seymour, so Ian had found us a place in Nagambie, a sleepy retirement town by a beautiful lake between Shepparton and Seymour. It had a population of about 1000 and was a much more agreeable 40 kilometres away from the army base. And now I'd passed my exams and achieved my birth count, I had managed to land a new job at Nagambie Bush Nursing Hospital.

Watching as Julie signed off my paperwork, I tried to put into words how grateful I was for all the help and support she had given me. I would never forget that she helped give me the confidence to believe in myself.

'It's my pleasure,' she smiled. 'You have a lovely manner about you, Beth. I would have you deliver my babies anytime.'

I felt quite emotional, and was embarrassed to feel my eyes tear up.

'That's what happens when you're on a ward pumping with oestrogen,' Julie teased. 'It turns you into a big sook.'

Chapter 5
The unthinkable

I had assumed downsizing from a 300-bed city hospital to a tiny bush hospital with just 14 beds would be an easy transition, but it proved a steep learning curve. The entire staff at Nagambie was just seven people, and with this much smaller staff, I soon discovered that issues which inevitably arise in any workplace among people of different ages, interests and experiences were magnified. If there was someone who didn't warm to you or disagreed with the way you did things then there was no escaping it. Added to the mix was my youth and inexperience and it wasn't long before that caused me trouble.

Only a month into the job, I found myself standing in front of the matron at Nagambie Hospital, Mauve, biting my lip nervously. Judging by the stern look on her face, I was about to be reprimanded.

'Last night Ruth called me away from my evening at home to help her with the woman who was in labour,' she said. 'Do you think it's acceptable I had to come in to finish your work?'

Thinking back, Ruth, the hospital's night midwife, had seemed a little frosty when I had made to leave the night before. I'd assumed it was the norm to hand over a labouring mother to the incoming staff when your shift was over – that was the way it had worked at PANCH. But PANCH was a much bigger place with several staff on duty at once. In leaving Ruth to cope alone, I realised too late that I'd made a big mistake.

It was mortifying to hear that she'd called my boss into the hospital to assist with the birth. 'I'm so sorry. I didn't know,' I stuttered. I'd assumed Ruth would call a GP to assist her, but clearly she had needed help before he arrived. I walked away feeling mortified, and agreed to apologise profusely to Ruth later. Looking back, I can't imagine what I was thinking – as a young, inexperienced graduate I clearly had a lot to learn.

Births were few and far between at Nagambie. The majority of my time was spent looking after the hospital's elderly patients, who were unable to care for themselves at home. Although I missed PANCH's busy maternity unit, this work was rewarding in its own way and I enjoyed caring for the old folk on the ward. They were stoic, perhaps by virtue of their generation, and rarely made a fuss. My eldest patient was a sweet lady in her late 90s who looked tiny tucked up in her hospital bed. She had been diagnosed with dementia some years before and whenever I walked past she would peer mischievously from under her sheet as if she was playing peekaboo.

One day I noticed something dark and grubby on her fingers. 'Granny, what have you been up to?' I asked her.

'Nothing, dear,' she said, trying to hide her hands from me. But when I got closer, I noticed a row of dark poo pebbles lined up on the windowsill. Oh, Granny! Helping her out of bed, I took her to the bathroom. 'There we go,' I said, gently washing her hands and arms with warm water and soap. Taking her back to the ward I sat her in a chair while I stripped and changed her bed linen.

'It wasn't me, dear,' she said calmly, smiling up at me as I removed the collection from the windowsill with gloved hands.

Shortly after this, Granny celebrated her 100th birthday and was photographed for the local paper, smiling with her telegram from the Queen. She was such a sweet, serene lady who dealt with the indignities of old age with real grace. I hoped that one day I would be able to do the same, but without the poo pebbles on the windowsill!

With such a small pool of staff, it was the responsibility of the nurses to arrange transport for the flying surgeon who would arrive from the Royal Melbourne Hospital every so often to carry out minor procedures at Nagambie. Ian often volunteered to drive to Mangalore airstrip, chase the kanga-roos off the runway and wait for the surgeon to land so he could taxi him to the hospital.

Not only was Ian quick to volunteer if the hospital needed help with something, he was also proving to be what I always knew he would be – a devoted, kind husband, and my best friend, someone I could always rely on. It was now 18 months since we'd got married and we'd started to daydream about having a family. I thought I'd like four children; Ian thought we had a good chance of having twins as he had twin sisters, and twin cousins from each of his mother's three brothers. I must say, I wasn't keen on the idea of twins – I'd seen how much harder they were on mothers, both at the birth and afterwards. One at a time would suit me just fine, I decided.

'I could come off the pill to see what happens?' I suggested.

What happened was that I immediately fell pregnant.

'At least we know it works!' Ian announced proudly when the doctor confirmed we were expecting.

I was young compared to many new mothers today – 23. But my age didn't cross my mind when I discovered I was going to have a baby, and whenever I thought about the tiny life growing inside me I could barely contain my delight. After all, I had witnessed countless times how wonderful and life-changing motherhood could be. Now it was my turn to experience that for myself.

Carrying my own baby was a great education in how gruelling pregnancy can be. I'd heard women complain about tiredness, sore boobs and morning sickness in their first trimester, but without going through it myself I could never really tell whether they were exaggerating, or truly empathise with their discomfort. Now I realised that something as small as a blueberry really could cause that much chaos – six weeks into my pregnancy just brushing my teeth would make me dry-retch. Thankfully, the feeling subsided as quickly as it came; nevertheless I spent a great deal of my first trimester feeling dog-tired and queasy, and that didn't subside until I was around 20 weeks.

Just as we were becoming accustomed to living in Nagambie, Ian was offered a Defence Department house in the larger town of Seymour, 30 kilometres away and only ten kilometres from Puckapunyal, so we decided to disrupt our lives yet further and move into it. It would mean an even shorter commute for Ian, and would give me the chance to work at a bigger hospital because Seymour Hospital had a vacancy for a sister. With my double certificate in nursing and midwifery I had the perfect qualifications. I arranged an interview and was offered the job the same day. A lot of army wives worked at the hospital, so I think management was used to staff coming and going, and the matron seemed relieved to have someone to cover the vacant four-night shift; plus she didn't seem to mind that I was pregnant.

Working nights is not ideal for a pregnant woman, but now that I was well into my second trimester I was feeling much better, and thankfully sleeping is something of a talent of mine – at home I would usually drift off as soon as my head hit the pillow. I was grateful to have this new job and was sure I could cope.

Mauve and my other colleagues were good people, but I'd never really gelled at Nagambie and often felt a bit isolated, so I wasn't sad to leave. At Seymour I would be using my midwifery skills again, and would work with a larger pool of staff, many closer to my age, including other army wives. I was confident it would be a better fit.

A few weeks into my new job, I was thoroughly enjoying interacting with mothers again, and realising how much I'd missed it. Despite being only about six months out of training, I was the sister-in-charge of the entire hospital. While this seemed daunting at first, if there were any problems I could always phone the doctor on call. My shifts ran from 11 pm to 7.30 am. I kept myself going by occasionally taking a power nap. I'd push my book or knitting to one side and rest my head on my arms for a quick sleep – I'd usually get 10 to 15 minutes before a patient bell would ring and I'd jump awake.

But while I took the odd catnap, the nightly sleeping spurts of a colleague of mine were ridiculous. One evening when I returned to the nurses' room after my fourth patient bell, I found Sleeping Beauty, a fellow army wife and nurse, out for the count on the sofa, curled up under a blanket she had brought in from home. It turned out that she had been snoozing there for the last two hours, remaining deathly still every time a bell went off.

It really irritated me that it was a nightly occurrence and she plain ignored the patient bells; meanwhile, the nurses' aide and I were doing the lion's share of the work. Did she really think she got paid to sleep?

After two weeks, I became cross enough to report it to the matron. I was just about to go home when she called me back into the office. There I found Sleeping Beauty, glaring at me.

'Now, what's this all about?' the matron asked us.

'She's just jealous that my husband is an officer and hers isn't!' my colleague announced. I was speechless!

'I'm not going to sit here listening to petty squabbles,' the matron announced. 'Beth, as the sister-in-charge this is something I would expect you to have sorted out yourself.' And with that she waved the pair of us out of her office.

Unsurprisingly the atmosphere was frosty between us after that. The whole episode taught me a valuable lesson. I hate confrontation, but I should have fronted up to my own battles and talked to Sleeping Beauty myself without involving the matron. At least she did stop nodding off on the job, and I didn't take any more catnaps – I wasn't game to after that!

Pregnancy definitely had its benefits. My concerned husband would often cook tea when he came home from work and send me back to bed after we'd eaten at night.

'Ian has hidden culinary skills,' I laughed to Mum and Faye during a weekend back in Cudgewa. 'He makes a mean spaghetti bolognaise!'

Faye had recently announced she was expecting and it was fun swapping pregnancy stories with her. Her due date was barely three months after mine, and it was nice to think our babies would be so close in age. I'd also chat to the mothers in my care about my own pregnancy, and we bonded over our shared experiences leading up to our big day.

My biggest challenge in those first weeks at Seymour was trying to work out the right time to call in the doctor for a birth. It seemed silly calling doctors away from their beds to do something I was perfectly capable of doing myself, but many of the mothers in the hospital were army wives with private insurance, so they were entitled to have a doctor deliver their baby and, just as it had been at PANCH, it was reiterated to us constantly that we had to get the doctor there in time.

The last thing I wanted was to call in a grumpy doctor who would then have to wait hours or, worse still, go home again, but judging how dilated a patient was without conducting a vaginal examination was tricky. While vaginal examinations can tell you exactly how far on in labour a woman is, they also carry the risk of passing infection to the baby. At both PANCH and Seymour they could only be done with a doctor's consent.

My other options were to put a finger up the woman's backside to feel the cervix through the anal wall, or to regularly palpate her stomach to feel how quickly the head was moving downwards. I always opted for the latter as it was obvious to me how uncomfortable an anal examination was for a woman in labour. I was also more in tune now with the sounds of a labouring woman and how her body reacted to breathing and movement as the labour progressed.

One night, I was pretty sure I'd got the timing spot on. My patient, Abigail, was pacing the floor in an agitated fashion, I'd called the doctor, and he'd promised to be there in 20 minutes. Suddenly Abigail's membranes ruptured and a gush of clear amniotic fluid cascaded down her legs.

I nodded at my nurse's aide to start warming the towels and asked Abigail to get on the bed. When I had started at Seymour I'd been relieved to learn that the hospital regulations didn't require women to be in stirrups when they gave birth, so Abigail was able to position herself more naturally, and adjust her body to deal with the pain.

To my surprise, once she was lying on the bed, I could immediately see her baby's head crowning. I could only imagine the scolding I'd get when the doctor arrived. With no time to waste, I positioned myself beside Abigail, and soon I had a wriggling baby in my hands. I was in the process of delivering the placenta when the doctor walked in, looking every inch a man who had just been summoned from his bed: he had his pyjama top on as a shirt and his hair was all ruffled. He peered at the baby in Abigail's arms.

'Looks like you have everything under control, sister,' he said to me with a yawn. 'Good job. I'll see you in the morning.'

In time I realised that plenty of doctors are relaxed or even relieved to miss a birth. By showing their face, they provide their 'private service', but instead of scrubbing up, they can head straight back to bed or their busy practice.

✳

As my eyes adjusted to the sunlight creeping through the closed blinds, I glanced at my bedside clock. It was 3 pm and I'd had six hours' sleep after returning home from my final night shift of the week. Lying in bed, I felt a weird sensation between my legs, like I was getting my period. When I went to the bathroom I found fresh blood in my pants.

I knew it wasn't uncommon to experience spotting but I didn't want to take any risks, so I immediately booked an appointment to see my GP the following day. Dr Bruce, a first-rate doctor, had been looking after my antenatal care, and I felt confident he would know what was going on. Now 25 weeks pregnant, I could still feel the baby moving and I'd seen situations in which a woman had been admitted to hospital with bleeding and gone home again to carry the pregnancy through to term. I didn't think too much about it and assumed I'd be one of those people.

To my relief, the bleeding had stopped by the time I went for my appointment the following morning. However, like many doctors in the 1970s, Dr Bruce didn't exactly sugar-coat things.

'Now you have to wait and see what happens,' he told me matter-of-factly. 'You need to go home and rest.' He prescribed valium, the drug of choice at that time for anything from high blood pressure to pre-eclampsia. 'Take three days' bed rest,' he instructed.

Hardly able to contemplate what might be happening, I did as I was told. For the next three days I remained in a valium haze, constantly lethargic, my emotions numbed. Although the drug kept me calm and I had no further bleeding, in hindsight I'm amazed I was given it. I didn't need to be drugged; I should have been told simply to rest up and to try to relax. But being the dutiful patient, I took my medicine. (Nowadays there is more emphasis on the effects of drugs on the foetus, and valium wouldn't be the first choice in such a situation.)

After my bed rest I returned to my normal routine, intending to get checked over by Dr Bruce the following week. I decided it would be safe to meet my friend Joy to go Christmas shopping in Bendigo. Joy had studied at Albury with Pam and me, and now lived and worked as a midwife 50 kilometres away in Heathcote. I thought it would be a welcome distraction from the stress of the previous week, but as we were walking back to Joy's car from the shops I felt a sort of peculiar pop inside me.

'I need to go to the bathroom,' I told Joy. 'I just felt something.'

Shutting myself in a shopping mall cubicle, I examined the thick sanitary pad I had put in my knickers as a precaution. There was no blood, but it seemed really wet. I took it back to the car and asked Joy to look at it. 'Do you think it's my membranes?' I asked her. Joy wasn't sure, but she immediately drove me back to her house and my car so I could head home and go to bed. I had been lying down for about half an hour when I felt fluid between my thighs. Scrabbling out of the sheets, I hitched up my nightie, to see blood streaming down my legs.

'Ian!' I yelled, as I pulled on my dressing gown and slippers. 'I need to go to hospital now!'

Even though it wasn't the closest hospital, I'd booked into Nagambie for the birth because I liked the care mothers-to-be received there. So, 25 minutes later, I was met by Ruth, the night midwife. She helped me to the maternity ward while Ian parked the car. I was still bleeding heavily and she called the doctor immediately.

It took Dr Bruce just 10 minutes to get to the hospital to examine me. 'Give her 100 milligrams of pethidine,' he ordered Ruth as he prepared to put an intravenous drip in my arm. 'We need to get her to Shepparton.' I knew Shepparton was the nearest obstetric referral centre.

Ruth injected the pain-relief drug into the top of my leg. While Dr Bruce was still trying to insert an intravenous canula into my arm, the ambulance driver arrived at the door with his trolley. I was overwhelmed by all that was happening to me and around me.

'What's going on?' I heard Ian ask.

Suddenly I was aware of a bulging sensation in my vagina.

'I can feel something,' I muttered, touching what I was sure was the baby's head.

There was some quick fumbling with the bed linen as Dr Bruce and Ruth checked to see what was going on. Hushed words were exchanged. I could feel our baby coming out and knew it was too soon. I was aware of Ian standing at the end of the bed in complete bewilderment. I thought I heard a few squeaks, but the small bundle was placed in a cot at the back of the room and quickly whisked away. There was no cry.

My baby had been born at 26 weeks.

The ambulance driver was instructed that he would not be needed and left. Struggling to keep my eyelids open, I felt completely dazed. I was aware of Ruth cleaning me up, but she didn't even mention the baby. My head swam as I tried to find the words to ask what had happened, but before I could say anything, the drug-induced sleep won.

As soon as I woke the next morning, my hands naturally went to my tummy. As I began to get my bearings and the confusion started to clear, a slow dread crept over me. I knew I had lost my baby. Struggling out of bed, I walked out of the ward and headed to the kitchen, where I found Mauve having breakfast. I sat down.

'Was my baby a boy or girl?' I asked.

'She was a girl,' Mauve answered.

'How long did she live for?'

'She didn't live,' she said.

I walked back to my room. It was the news I had expected, yet I was sure I'd heard my baby make a noise. Climbing back into bed, I felt hollow and empty. I lay there for a while, drifting in and out of a fitful sleep, when suddenly I was aware of a middle-aged man standing in the doorway. He walked over to the bed and handed me an envelope.

'I'm Greg from the funeral directors,' he said. 'I'll be looking after things.'

When he left I opened the envelope. Inside was a bill for $80 for 'Baby McRae', the little girl I'd planned to name Desma Lorraine.

Suddenly it was all very real, heartbreakingly real. I clutched my belly and howled with grief. It was just so clinical and horrible – I hadn't even seen my baby. There would be no funeral, nothing. This was the end.

When Ian arrived soon afterwards, I was inconsolable. 'I want to go home,' I told him, tears streaming down my cheeks. 'Get me out of this place.'

Looking back now I can hardly fathom the heartlessness of how I was treated. There was no offer of counselling or condolences by the hospital, and to allow the undertaker to deliver a bill to my bedside was unforgiveable. The awful thing is that it wasn't a case of me being treated particularly badly – it was just the way things were done in those days.

During my midwifery training we had been told not to dwell on death. As students we were kept away from women who had lost babies and mostly they were transferred to wards in the hospital well away from the maternity unit, away from the crying newborns and clucky mothers. You just didn't talk about such a loss. Suddenly I understood how terrible that denial was for the woman concerned. It makes you feel as though your baby does not matter. As though your baby never really existed.

✳

As soon as I arrived home I called Mum. Ian had to get back to work and he seemed at a loss to know how to comfort me. He was so used to me being in control, but right now I couldn't hide how fragile I felt.

'We'll leave now,' Mum told me with a wobble in her voice. 'We'll be with you before teatime.'

When my parents arrived, laden with flowers and home-cooked meals, I was holding a laundry basket filled with blood-stained sheets.

'Give me that,' Mum ordered. 'You sit down and rest.'

For the next few days she fussed over me, busying herself with the washing and other chores while Dad made me cups of tea. While my parents were not demonstrative by nature, their actions spoke louder than words. It meant the world to have them there. They were with us for about a week and when they had to leave, I knew I must try to get on with life. But one thing was eating away at me. Apart from the undertaker's bill, I had no paperwork to acknowledge my baby's birth or death. During my midwifery training we had learnt that a baby was viable at 20 weeks. So why hadn't my old colleagues registered my baby?

'It is twenty weeks,' my friend Joy confirmed. 'You need to tell them.'

So, plucking up the courage, two months later I drove to Nagambie to have it out with the matron. When Mauve ushered me into the office, I told her straight out.

'I'm sorry, Beth, but we can't register the baby you lost,' she replied. 'A baby needs to be 28 weeks to be viable.'

As she folded her arms, I felt an uncontrollable surge of anger rising inside of me. I rarely show my emotions, but suddenly I was consumed by the injustice. I knew she was wrong. I was standing in a registered maternity hospital that didn't even know the viability rules. It was disgusting.

'I know what the rules are and I suggest you read up on them,' I fumed. 'Nagambie is no different to the rest of Victoria and you need to register my baby's birth.'

I was prepared to take my fight to a lawyer, but eight weeks later a letter dropped into our mailbox from the Births, Deaths and Marriages office. It was a shallow victory but an important one for me, to help me process my grief. I wanted my baby's life to count despite the fact it had been cut short.

Losing Desma was one of the most harrowing experiences of my life, but if any good came out of the heartache, it was that from then on I became a more compassionate midwife. In later years, when women in my care were in the same awful situation, I would do everything I could to help and support them. Women who have a stillborn baby are often frightened that he or she will look dead or abnormal. So instead of whisking the body away, I always make sure I stand with the baby in my arms to show the mother how peaceful her child looks. Then, if she wants to hold her baby, I will gently place the baby in her arms.

'You'll never get this moment again, so think carefully about what you would like to do,' is the advice I always give parents.

More often than not, parents choose to spend a little time with their child and are grateful that they did, that they had the chance to say goodbye.

Chapter 6
A new start

In the months that followed, just walking down the street and catching sight of a pregnant woman would make my stomach churn. As my baby bump shrank, I couldn't help thinking Faye's would be growing. I did my best to prepare myself for watching her experience all the stages and joys of having a baby when I had lost mine. But as Ian and I had headed home to Cudgewa to spend Christmas with my family, I had to admit I was dreading the prospect of coming face to face with Faye for the first time since I'd lost Desma.

As soon as I saw Faye, I knew we were both just as anxious about upsetting each other.

'You look lovely,' I said. Her worried face relaxed into a smile. I was relieved to find I could chat about her second trimester without feeling the familiar ache. No matter what I'd been through, this was Faye's time, completely separate from mine, and she was entitled to be happy and excited. For now babies were off my wish list. The pain of Desma's still-birth was too raw to try again any time soon and I'd already gone back on the pill. That decision helped me through my sister's pregnancy.

That Christmas, I vowed not to let myself become miserable. I threw myself into helping Mum as she rustled up her favourite seasonal roast turkey with potatoes and veggies, followed by the traditional Christmas pudding, trifle, pavlova, ice-cream and hot custard. After lunch we had a long walk and a swim in the creek. I could feel myself slowly accepting a little of the pain I had been trying to keep at bay.

These relaxed days with my close family helped me to regain some of my equilibrium, and by the New Year I felt almost ready to bite the bullet and return to work. Just like Faye, my night-duty colleagues trod carefully when they first encountered me in the hospital, giving me sympathetic glances or making carefully worded enquiries after my health. But I had been brought up in a family that did not encourage wallowing. Instead of dwelling on the past, I wanted to get on with things, keep busy on the ward. For this reason I found it surprisingly easy to detach my own experience from those of the mothers and babies I delivered. As Desma's due date of 3 March came and went, I determinedly pushed any feelings aside. Allowing myself time to think about it and dwelling on what might have been might cause me to tumble back down the rabbit hole, and why do that to myself?

A little over two months later, Mum called to say Faye had given birth to a healthy baby girl, called Andrea. I promised to call Faye as soon as she was home from hospital, but a few days later I was woken by a mid-afternoon phone call from Paul.

'Faye's had a fit,' he said. 'They've transferred her to Melbourne for investigation.'

The doctors' first concern was that Faye was suffering an eclamptic fit, although she had no signs of pre-eclampsia, a condition that can affect pregnant and post-partum women, causing high blood pressure, protein in the urine and some-times oedema – swelling due to excess fluid being retained by the body. While an EEG (a test to examine electrical pulses in the brain) had highlighted unusual activity, there was no sign of protein in Faye's urine. With no history of epilepsy either, her condition remained a mystery. After a week of observation she was allowed home to Mum and Dad's place with anti-seizure medication.

Staying at the farm should have done Faye the world of good but a week later Mum still seemed worried. 'I don't think she's coping very well,' she told me on the phone. 'She seems down.'

The obvious solution was for me to take some time off to go and help out Faye, so that afternoon I made the four-hour drive to Cudgewa. When I arrived in the early evening,

Faye was sleeping and Mum was feeding Andrea. As soon as I saw my tiny niece with her beautiful head of soft dark hair, I felt overwhelmed with love.

When Faye woke up and we started talking, it was clear that she had lost confidence in herself.

'The medication makes me so tired,' she told me tearfully. 'I can't even look after my own daughter.'

We gave her strict orders to go to bed every time tiredness engulfed her and I took over Andrea's feeding, changing and bathing, doing anything I could to help lighten the load. If Andrea cried at 3 am, I would crawl out of bed to give her expressed milk in a bottle. Each morning I changed her nappy, dressed her in a clean outfit and handed her to Faye for breastfeeding. Just as I hoped, a couple of nights of good sleep helped restore her confidence no end. Slowly but surely she seemed to be relaxing and enjoying peaceful moments with her daughter. Once I was sure all was well, I returned to Seymour, feeling happy that I had been able to help my sister and surprisingly boosted by catching a glimpse of what it would be like to have a baby of my own.

Back at work, I began to think about my future. Seven months had passed since I'd lost Desma and, if I was honest with myself, sometimes I still felt as though I was on autopilot. Our jobs and their conflicting hours meant Ian and I barely spoke some days. In years gone by we'd always made time to do things together and I wanted to get back to those days, which seemed to have been much more carefree and certainly happier. But that would never happen while I worked nights.

A few weeks later I was in a delivery suite with a labour-ing mother when I got chatting to a doctor I worked with regularly and he told me about a vacancy at his surgery for a practice nurse, working office hours. 'You should let me know if you're interested,' he said.

Maybe a break from the labour ward and some sociable working hours were what I needed. I decided on the spot to apply and he promised to organise an interview. A week later the job was mine and in January 1977 I started work at Bryce, Russell & Richards in Seymour.

In my new job, while there was always something to do, the pace was much slower and that took some getting used to. Helping the doctor with dressings, small procedures and ordering the stock was not the most exciting life, but the hours did work for Ian and me. With more evenings together we enjoyed meals out as well as trips to the movies. I appreciated the fact that no one at the surgery knew about my 'tragedy', too. Life began to feel better and even light-hearted again.

However, my time at Bryce, Russell & Richards turned out to be brief. As long as Ian served in the forces we were at the whim of the army, and in July he was posted to Watsonia in Melbourne, 100 kilometres away. I felt a little embarrassed that I had to hand my notice in after just three months, but I hoped that it meant I could get a job back at PANCH.

*

Happily, three years after leaving PANCH, I returned as a general midwife and second-in-charge on the private ante-natal and postnatal ward. The 30-bed ward, where I'd learnt my first lessons to become a midwife, was now run by a straight-talking Scotswoman called Rhonda.

In a short time, so much had changed. Demand feeding and rooming-in, which allowed babies to stay by their mother's side, were now routine on the ward and Rhonda was keen to improve the holistic side of maternity care.

'Women cope best giving birth when they are supported and well-informed,' Rhonda said. 'It's our job to help them understand everything that is happening to them and encour-age them to make their own decisions.'

I immediately warmed to Rhonda, and I was impressed that she had no qualms about speaking her mind if she didn't agree with a doctor's decision. In my first week I saw her challenging a GP who seemed impatient to induce a mother for no other reason than that it was convenient for him.

'What do you wanna do that for?' she asked him. 'Let nature take its course!'

Rhonda's other big passion was breastfeeding. She wouldn't think twice about spending an hour with a mother who needed help to get started. 'Just let the baby open its mouth,' she would say. 'Take your baby to the breast, not the breast to the baby.'

Rhonda wholeheartedly believed breast was best – I'd never heard anyone talk so passionately about breastfeeding before. She'd tell the mothers, 'Your milk is wonderful for your baby. It gives your baby the best nutrition and helps keep allergies at bay.'

Working with Rhonda was inspiring every day and over the next few months we became good friends as well as colleagues.

Organising the maternity ward and keeping things running smoothly was a big part of my job and I often answered calls from the delivery suite, asking which room they should admit a new mother and baby to. During my first week I recognised a familiar voice on the line. 'Julie?' I asked. My old mentor was still here at PANCH! Half an hour later I was working by her side, admitting a new mother to room 14. Noticing a soggy lump of biscuit on the woman's bedside table, I asked her why it was there.

'It's for the baby,' the woman replied. I laughed along for a moment, until I realised she was serious. 'What do you mean?' I asked.

'The baby likes it,' she said. 'I dunk it in my tea and give it to him.'

After explaining that newborn babies definitely should not eat milk arrowroot biscuits, I cleared away the soggy remains. Just when I thought I had seen and heard everything. But it was a reminder that we should never assume anything with new mothers, or any patient, for that matter. And that in a maternity ward there is never a dull moment!

Once mother and child were settled into their room, I was able to catch up with Julie by the nurses' desk.

When I told her about all the changes I'd noticed, she filled me in on some other welcome updates. 'We've stopped using stirrups for normal births and even the charge nurse is coming round to the fact that enemas should be optional. I think everyone is relieved.'

Now that I was more experienced, I was keen to take a leaf out of Julie's book when it came to mentoring the midwifery students. Remembering all too well my own uncertainty in getting to grips with the skills of delivery, I made it my mission to go out of my way to help the student midwives, so I was constantly on the lookout for antenatal patients who would be open to students testing their palpating skills on them.

One expectant mother who loved students to visit her was Margi, who was 30 weeks pregnant with her first child. A 28-year-old hairdresser, Margi had been admitted with a condition called placenta praevia, which means the placenta embeds into the lower segment of the uterus and may cover the cervix. Having been diagnosed with grade 4, when the placenta completely covers the cervix and there is an increased risk of heavy bleeding, hospital was definitely the safest place for Margi. She would remain with us for two months until an obstetrician delivered her baby by caesarean section at 38 weeks. Despite this, Margi remained one of the chirpiest patients on the ward and one quiet evening she beckoned for me to pull up a chair. 'Let me do your hair while you have ten minutes free,' she said.

I was amused to see she'd stashed her equipment bag under the bed and soon she was producing numerous brushes and sprays. My short hair didn't require much styling but she set to work combing, teasing and spraying away. I think it gave her a welcome break from the boredom of bed rest. Over the next few weeks our wards began to look very chic as several midwives and most of the mothers received their own makeovers.

When Margi reached 38 weeks, she was whisked off to theatre and I made a silent prayer she and her baby would be okay. Arriving for work the following day, I headed straight to room 15. Inside, I found Margi nursing a beautiful baby girl. 'This is Mandy,' she said with a smile. Of course, she'd already styled her daughter's hair, caressing her few dark strands into a cute comb-over.

One morning as I was doing my usual morning rounds on the ward, I was summoned to the desk to answer a call from Julie in the delivery suite.

'We're sending over a new arrival,' she said. 'She'll need a lot of support, Beth. She lost her baby a few hours ago.'

My heart immediately went out to this poor woman, who'd given birth to a stillborn baby at 36 weeks. By now PANCH had become much more progressive in training all its staff how to treat women who'd lost their babies. It was at last recognised that mourning parents should spend time with their child, and the hospital offered to give parents keepsakes such as footprints and locks of hair. We were encouraged to speak with the bereaved parents openly about their loss.

After the insensitive treatment I had endured at Nagambie Hospital after losing my own baby, I thought carefully about everything I could do to help another mother through this heartbreaking time. Quickly making up a bed in a private room, well away from the cries of other babies, I removed the cot from the room and set out a glass, a jug of water and a box of tissues.

Dropping in to visit later on, I found her curled up in bed with her husband next to her. Both looked pale and drawn, their eyes red and puffy from crying.

'I'm so sorry about what happened to you today,' I told them after introducing myself. 'If you need anything, let me know. I'll leave you to settle in.'

When I checked back a little later, the woman was by herself. I asked her how she was.

'Not good,' she said. 'I feel like I'm living a nightmare.'

'Did you get some time with your baby?' I asked her softly.

'Yes', she said, blowing her nose with a tissue. 'We said goodbye to her just before I came over here.'

'If you want more time with her, please let me know,' I said. 'I can also sit with you and explain the paperwork. Give the bell a ring if there's anything I can help you with.'

Although the woman and her husband chose not to see their baby again, she did take up my offer to help her fill in the registration paperwork, and she opened up a little more about her pain and grief, feelings I knew all too well. This was the first time I'd been able to help a bereaved mother since losing my own daughter. It felt good to be able to help someone even a little bit with the terrible loss they were feeling, even just to be there to listen. I rarely spoke about my personal experience in these situations simply because, understandably, the person experiencing his or her own raw grief is not interested at that moment in what has happened to someone else. The pain, as I know, is so terrible and so all encompassing. Instead I would focus on listening and doing whatever I could to help.

March 1978 brought with it an exciting new opportunity for me when a clinical educator's role came up at PANCH. I applied, and my enthusiasm must have been obvious as I immediately got the job. I welcomed the change and the challenge – and the pay rise. The previous October Ian and I had bought a three-bedroom house in the Melbourne suburb of Greensborough, and we were sharing the mortgage costs between us.

I still remembered my own first days as a graduate nurse as if it were yesterday and here I was, four years later, officially overseeing PANCH's latest batch of midwife recruits. My job was to work alongside them until they had earned their double scrubs – three supported deliveries with a mentor midwife. After that they would deliver babies by themselves with a senior colleague watching.

One day a clearly distressed student walked into my office. Trying her best not to cry, Chloe told me how her first unassisted delivery had ended. After catching the baby, she had been shocked to spot a second, unexpected newborn making a rapid entry into the world. Her supervising midwife had reacted quickly, making a grab for the baby, but it had already plummeted head first into the stainless steel bucket on the floor.

Chloe let out a sob. 'What if she has a fractured skull?'

Although I kept my face composed, I was horrified for her. My worst student nightmare had come true – but for Chloe. Nevertheless, there was no point distressing herself any further. First we had to find out what had happened to the baby. After contacting the nursery, I was told the second twin had been sent for an X-ray and, despite her dramatic entry into the world, she was none the worse for wear. Poor Chloe! I told her how frightened I'd also been of that happening, and that she must move on, and not allow herself to live in fear of the same thing happening again.

A year later PANCH expanded their commitment to our training program by appointing a senior midwifery lecturer from the Royal Women's Hospital in Melbourne, one of the best maternity teaching centres for midwifery and medical students.

Anne had a wonderful gift for inspiring her students and talked about birth as a magical and wonderful experience for women. Often I would creep into her lectures as she urged a new generation of midwives to listen to mothers' needs and strive to make their experiences of giving birth as positive as possible.

'Women should be able to make requests about how they want to be treated in pregnancy and labour,' Anne concluded. 'It's up to us as midwives to come forward and be advocates for all women having babies. Give them informed choices.'

As well as delivering her own impassioned lectures, Anne would regularly invite guest speakers to address the students. One lunchtime she introduced a speaker from the Childbirth Education Association (CEA), a group championing women's rights to have an informed birth. The CEA's reputation at the time was a bit hippy-ish, and I was a little sceptical going into the lecture, but hearing their representative's perspective was surprisingly engaging.

'Lying on your back is a very uncomfortable way to give birth,' she told the room. 'There need to be more choices for women in labour, for them to be mobile, to be able to squat or stand.'

I was inclined to agree. Since returning to PANCH I'd noticed a big difference in the way women laboured when they were free of stirrups and were able to move into a supported squat position thanks to the latest adjustable birthing beds. Allowing mothers to move like this and sway their hips seemed to aid the baby's descent through the pelvis. While mothers at PANCH were expected to stay on the bed for labour, it did give me hope that in the future they would be able to choose to walk around the room while they laboured, and squat or even stand for their baby's birth. It seemed a matter of common sense: gravity would then help the baby to come out. If a woman is lying on a bed on her back, her pelvis naturally tilts upwards, and therefore actually impedes the baby's descent through the cervix and out of the vagina.

One day I joined the students on an excursion to a new birthing unit at the Royal Women's Hospital, especially designed to provide mothers with a home birth environment. As soon as I walked in I could see why labouring women would love it here. Stainless steel birthing beds and trolleys of equipment had been replaced with double beds and a lounge suite. All the instruments, resuscitation gear and gas were hidden away behind cupboards – to the point where it reminded me more of a comfy hotel suite than a hospital. It felt homely, but with the added reassurance of knowing you were in fact in the hospital, should there be an emergency.

As Anne said, 'This is how childbirth should be.'

While I admired Anne's ability to find interesting and informative guests, one day I wasn't so impressed by the speaker. The woman was a spokesperson for the Association of Relinquishing Mothers, a charitable group set up to support women who have lost a child or children to adoption. As she spoke from the heart about how midwives should show empathy to women in this situation, I found myself irrationally irritated. I knew she was right – I knew firsthand the importance of empathising, showing compassion and understanding to anyone who has lost a child – but I didn't want to listen to her. It was as if she was advocating self-pity, and

I couldn't stand that kind of thing. Afterwards, I bumped into Rhonda in the corridor.

'How did the talk go?' she asked.

'Hmm,' I replied. 'There was a lot of wallowing. Some people just need to move on from what's happened to them.'

Rhonda studied me for a moment.

'The trouble with you, Beth, is you have some unresolved grief,' she said softly.

Immediately I felt defensive. It was three years since I'd lost Desma. Wasn't I getting on with life? But when I thought about it later, her words struck a chord. Whether I liked to admit it or not, in my heart I knew that the real reason I'd felt irritated with the woman from the Association of Relinquishing Mothers was that her subject was too close to the bone. Listening to her describing the anguish of giving up a child reminded me of the pain I had worked so hard to push to the back of my mind.

Today bereaved parents are offered counselling and there are many opportunities for them to discuss their grief. Back then, to do so was neither encouraged nor promoted as a sensible or useful. Nonetheless, my common sense told me then that maybe it was a good idea to acknowledge the pain once in a while.

Working with Anne, I felt we were part of something really progressive: new, better ways of supporting women in childbirth. I felt enlightened to be so involved in teaching and promoting these new methods, and would go to work fired up with enthusiasm for my job. So the last thing I wanted to hear was that the army was suddenly planning to transfer Ian back to Puckapunyal.

'But we've just bought a house!' I protested when Ian broke the news. 'Now you'll have to travel all that way again.'

When he contemplated the 100-kilometre commute, Ian had a think about our future, and after some soul-searching – we had a $36,000 mortgage, after all – he decided he'd ask for a discharge from the army and look for something completely new on civvy street.

It was a daunting prospect, but we were happy with our life in Melbourne. 'I think the army has made the decision for you,' I agreed.

We need not have worried. Ian is highly skilled, thanks to his army mechanic background, and it wasn't long before he found a position with the Gas and Fuel Corporation of Victoria. As a motor mechanic in their research and development team, he would be helping to upgrade motor vehicles to LP Gas and Natural Gas. It was groundbreaking work in Australia and a great challenge.

'Plus I don't have to salute the boss every day!' he said.

In August 1979 I decided to join the local branch of the Childbirth Education Association in Greensborough. Walking down the front path of a mudbrick house, I wasn't surprised to find an overgrown garden complete with statues of sun goddesses and wind chimes. 'Very CEA,' I thought.

I must admit that I didn't expect to learn much. I knew I liked what the CEA stood for, but my motivation was more that *I* could help them. As a clinical educator and having worked so closely with Rhonda and Anne, I thought I was up-to-date with all the latest thinking on birthing. But by the time I left that day, I felt my eyes had been opened.

The group was run by Geri, a qualified teacher on maternity leave who demonstrated an impressive know-ledge of childbirth. Just like Anne and Rhonda, she wanted labouring women to be proactive in expressing their needs and expectations.

'That's why it is essential to have a birth plan,' Geri said. 'The plan outlines what you do and don't want for your birth. It states that you expect to be asked before being given pain relief, that you are informed before an episiotomy, that the baby stays with you after birth . . .'

While I was a strong believer in listening to the women in my care, I had never thought to encourage them to make a birth plan. What a great idea to impart to the students! Over the years I had seen a lot of women in labour blindly doing whatever they were told by a bossy midwife or doctor. They often seemed scared and vulnerable. After all, giving birth is not something you do every day, and the experts must know best. But now Anne and I were encouraging a new generation of midwives to work differently. I loved watching the students as they encouraged the women in their care and helped them to understand the process. In response, the women seemed empowered, more at ease with what was happening to them and able to cope better with the pain of labour.

After that first CEA meeting, I was keen to go back, and each time I attended over the coming months I learnt something new – which was just as well, because I was pregnant again!

Chapter 7
Keeping everything crossed

Five years after losing my baby I finally felt ready to give pregnancy another shot, and within two months of coming off the pill I was expecting again.

I was eight weeks along when, in March 1980, Virgil, an obstetric GP from PANCH, confirmed all was well. I'd chosen Virgil to be my doctor because not only was he great at his job but he was gentle, kind and never overpowering with his opinions. I liked the way he talked labouring women through every step of their birth.

'If you have any worries, just let me know immediately,'

he told me when I explained my past history. 'You can always grab me at work.'

Having lost my first baby in such heartbreaking circumstances, I knew it was going to be difficult not to feel paranoid about every pain and twinge of this pregnancy. But I was determined to try hard to stay upbeat. My life mantra has always been to think positive. I really believe that if you focus on the bad, you'll invite bad things into your life. But if you focus on the good, you open yourself up to all the positive things that can happen.

As I reached the all-important 12-week mark, Ian and I began to reflect on the kind of birth we wanted. I would have loved to have had my baby in the fabulous birthing centre I had seen at the Women's Hospital, but it was not to be. When I made inquiries, I was disappointed to learn they didn't accept anyone with an abnormal obstetric history.

'It doesn't matter where you have your baby as long as you have good people around you,' Anne reassured me. 'You can cherrypick who you like at PANCH.'

So as I toured the maternity unit with my students, I had no qualms about selecting my 'dream team'. First off the list was the surly obstetrician who could hardly bring himself to speak to patients and whom I had seen poking and prodding mothers with little care for how it must make them feel.

Then there was the veteran midwife with a penchant for performing rectal examinations on labouring mothers. While we all knew that too many vaginal examinations could increase the risk of infection, she wasn't interested in

113

estimating how far along the women were using patience and observation. On several occasions I'd seen her waltz in, grab the gloves and announce, 'I'm going to check you,' then shove her finger up a poor woman's backside.

'She's missed her calling, she should have been a proctologist,' I said to Rhonda after witnessing yet another poor expectant mother yelping with shock and pain.

Next off my list were any thoughtless, apathetic midwives. A first-time mother in particular needs constant reassurance, because her labour tends to progress with an overwhelming intensity. It troubled me to see some colleagues silently examining women and then leaving the room without giving them even a hint of encouragement. When women feel supported, they are able to cope better with pain.

'It won't be like this forever,' Anne told me. 'The midwives we're training now will be the ones who change the culture.'

One of Anne's goals was to convince PANCH to introduce midwife-taught antenatal classes so that mums-to-be were equipped with coping techniques for their labour. While the hospital physiotherapy department ran a good antenatal class, it concentrated on the physical impact of pregnancy and labour. There was so much more a midwife could add. All pregnant women would benefit from learning relaxation techniques as well as being given advice on how to look after their newborns and learning all the advantages of breastfeeding.

In the meantime I was delighted to be asked to teach antenatal classes for the CEA. The courses were held one evening a week for six weeks in a spare classroom at La Trobe University. I learnt the ropes by sitting in on another class, and was fascinated by the breathing techniques the CEA recommended. Learning to breathe to manage pain seemed like a very natural way of coping with the contractions.

'As the contraction starts to come, breathe in through your nose and out through your mouth,' I explained to the women in my own class. 'Concentrate on doing that as deeply and slowly as possible, and find an inner place. Imagine you are lying on a beach on warm sand, and as you breathe in you are sinking comfortably into the sand. Then, as you breathe out, feel how relaxed you are. By the time you reach the peak of the contraction, you will be in a comfortable zone.'

Another important aspect of my class was educating expectant mums on the advantages of breastmilk, explaining that it is full of natural antibiotics and how good it is for a baby's immune system. Then I would take a leaf out of Rhonda's book to explain the most effective and pain-free ways to breastfeed. Breastfeeding should be a natural process, but around the fourth day after the birth, when new mothers sometimes feel a little 'blue' due to hormonal changes, things can go wrong and it can be very tempting for a worried, vulnerable woman to decide she's failed with breastfeeding and give up. I reassure them that difficulty breastfeeding for the first time is common, but it is almost always temporary, and encourage them to persist.

'If it hurts, the baby likely isn't attached properly,' I'd explain. 'Take the baby off and start again . . .'

I found the shared excitement of chatting to other mothers-to-be gave me reassurance myself. Another pregnant mum revealed her story of having a stillborn baby at 28 weeks and that she'd gone on to have her next child without any issues.

'Having Heidi was such a positive thing,' she said as her two-year-old daughter played at her feet. 'It was as though our world started turning again. We had a new life after the heartbreak.'

As she spoke I could feel myself choke up, but this time in a good way. Her story reinforced my own hope. This time I would have a healthy baby too.

The beginning of the 1980s brought rapid advancements in medical and obstetric technology. One of the most talked about was ultrasound, then a new, hi-tech way of studying a foetus's development inside the womb. How amazing that a special transducer for the stomach could convert soundwaves into an image of the baby. This grainy picture allowed obstetricians to measure the size of the foetus, check its growth and predict an accurate due date. Not only would shock twins become a thing of the past, the ultrasound could also pick up all sorts of foetal abnormalities.

By now I was 18 weeks pregnant, and my growing bump and the occasional flutter in my tummy reassured me my baby was thriving. However, an ultrasound would tell me for sure. With the technology not yet commonplace in many hospitals, I made an appointment with Hugh Robinson, a Scottish doctor based at the Women's, who was one of the top obstetric ultrasonographers in Victoria. 'If there's something wrong with our baby, he'll find it,' I told Ian.

As I lay on the examination bed in Dr Robinson's office, I held Ian's hand tightly and watched as he squeezed jelly on my stomach and began to move a probe across my bump. Grainy shapes that reminded me of a weather map appeared on the screen.

'There are the baby's hands,' Dr Robinson told us. 'Now let's have a look at the heartbeat.'

As he moved the transducer I could see a pulsating movement on the screen.

'Everything looks wonderful,' he confirmed. 'Your baby looks just right for eighteen weeks.'

I could hardly speak for the relief. 'Thank you,' I eventually murmured as a grinning Ian shook the doctor's hand.

As flutters in my belly turned into clear kicks over the next four weeks, Ian and I began to discuss our birth plan. After being so out of it at Desma's birth, I certainly didn't want any form of pain relief. I didn't want to be induced either.

'And I'd like to be involved in the birth,' Ian said. 'I want to learn what I can do to help now, rather than you having to tell me as it happens.'

After watching far too many hapless fathers floundering during the birth of their child, I wasn't about to look this gift horse in the mouth – I promptly booked us onto a course of six CEA classes that would begin when I was 32 weeks pregnant.

'We'll learn everything and you'll have no excuse to faint,' I teased Ian.

As 26 weeks – the gestation at which I'd lost Desma – came and went, I began to allow myself to feel excited. Up until now I had held off decorating a room for the baby in fear of jinxing things. But as my confidence grew and I continued to feel the sensation of moving inside me, I began to prepare the nursery.

Pride of place was the beautiful white cradle Ian's brother-in-law, Rex, had made us. We lined it with a special mattress made from feather-light tea-tree paperbark flakes, purchased from a specialist baby shop. The word on the maternity ward was that this was the best mattress you could buy: it was 'breathable' and moulded to the baby like today's memory foam. Next, I whipped up a pair of lime-green curtains and a matching doona on my Singer sewing machine. The final touch was a chest of drawers painted white to match the cradle.

'All we need now is our baby,' I said.

At 27 weeks, the little mite was making its presence felt, occasionally waking me in the night with a kicking frenzy. Apart from being tired, I felt good. So good, in fact, that I felt confident to remain at work, continuing to oversee the student midwives. With one school year almost complete, and another group halfway through, there was more than enough to keep me occupied. Anne was flat out preparing for an incoming group of 10 students in two weeks' time. I promised her I'd remain at work for another six weeks.

That way I could see this new school year of midwives through their first month of training.

Up until now I'd had no spotting, so when I noticed a bloody discharge one morning, I couldn't help but feel a spark of panic. Spying Virgil on the labour ward, I asked him to examine me as soon as he could. After palpating my stomach and listening to the baby's heart, he used a speculum and light to look at my cervix.

'I can see some mucus, but that's normal at this stage,' he said. 'If it gets worse let me know, but it's probably nothing to worry about.'

Relieved, I went back to work, but I took things more slowly. There was no more spotting – until two weeks later. On Father's Day, of all days, there was fresh blood in my knickers. At 5.30 pm that Sunday I reluctantly called Virgil.

'It might be nothing, but if you see more blood go straight to the hospital,' he told me. 'I'm about to go to a birthday party, but tell the staff to page me if they need me to come in.'

I went to bed and tried not to panic. Just after 9 pm I was aware of the uncomfortable sensation of my stomach tightening. It should have been far too early for contractions – I was only 29 weeks pregnant – yet the feeling kept coming and going. With a feeling of dread, I asked Ian to drive me to hospital.

We arrived at PANCH just before 10 pm, less than 12 hours before I was due to welcome 10 rookie midwives to the ward. I headed straight to the Emergency Department.

They wasted no time in transferring me to Maternity, where I was met by Frances, a midwife I knew well. She didn't seem entirely convinced I was in labour.

'Are you sure it's not Braxton Hicks?' she asked, helping me up onto a birthing bed. 'I had those when I was pregnant and they were quite painful.'

Braxton Hicks are contractions of the uterine muscles, which occur during the pregnancy but don't signal labour.

'It could be nothing,' I said curtly. 'I just want to get checked and then we can go home.'

Her reaction did give me pause – was I wasting everyone's time? But I badly needed reassurance after my last experience, so there was no way I was going to leave now. I wanted nothing left to chance.

She left the room to ring Virgil. All of a sudden I felt a pop sensation, followed by a flood of wetness between my legs. 'Quick, press the button,' I told Ian.

'I've ruptured my membranes,' I said as Frances came running into the room. I told Ian to get my bag from the car – I knew then I was there to stay. I felt weirdly calm – it was almost like an out-of-body experience. And I kept telling myself that I was four weeks further on than I'd been with Desma, which would make the world of difference to the baby's condition.

Ian returned five minutes later, accompanied by Virgil, who immediately began to scrub up. By now the spasm in my lower abdomen had increased to what felt like the worst menstrual cramps imaginable. Remembering the advice

I had dished out in antenatal classes, I tried to stay in the moment, breathing through each contraction. The only good thing about the pain was that it was all-consuming, making it impossible for me to panic anymore about the baby being born 10 weeks early. As soon as the contraction subsided, Virgil carried out an internal examination.

'You're fully dilated and ready for delivery,' he confirmed.

As another gripping pain overcame me, I was barely aware of the flurry of midwives getting ready for a premature birth.

'We need to put you into stirrups to see what's going on,' Virgil said. I didn't protest. I was aware of Ian sitting beside me, looking helpless. He had not attended a single CEA class yet and apart from stroking my hair and telling me he loved me, he seemed at a loss to know what to do.

'I can see the top of the baby's head,' Virgil announced. 'Beth, I would like to cut an episiotomy so there's less pressure.'

'Okay,' I gasped. The incision came with a mild sting.

'Now I want you to push,' Virgil instructed.

The excruciating cramps were replaced with a sensation of fullness spreading through my vagina and bottom – I felt as though I was going to explode.

'The head is out,' Virgil confirmed. One more agonising push and I felt my baby slip free.

'It's a girl! Here she is!' he said, lifting a tiny, bright pink baby up between my legs and onto my stomach. The first things I noticed were her gangly arms and legs. Then her little face scrunched up and she let out a cry. As tears of relief trickled down my cheeks, I cradled my baby to my chest. Thank God she was alive and breathing.

'You got your Father's Day present!' I said to Ian.

As we both gazed at the daughter we had decided to name Lauren Elizabeth, I was aware of Frances lingering. She stepped forward and took my little girl. 'I'm sorry but we need to get her to the special care nursery,' she said. I knew this was routine care for a premature baby, but seeing Lauren wheeled from the room was hard.

'Go with her,' I told Ian.

I lay there trying not to cry as Virgil delivered the placenta and then stitched up my episiotomy. Ian arrived back in the room just as my legs were freed from the stirrups.

'She's 1490 grams, that's three pounds four,' he blurted out. 'She's on oxygen and the paediatrician wants to transfer her to the Royal Children's Hospital in case her condition worsens and she needs help breathing.'

I knew from experience that the next six hours could go either way. Although she had appeared to be breathing well at birth, there was a chance she could deteriorate. There was no way I was going to wait around for my sponge bath.

'Pass me my dressing gown,' I said, throwing back the covers and attempting to get off the high bed. 'I'd like to go to the nursery now.'

Although Frances didn't try to stop me, she did insist I take a wheelchair. Ian pushed me into the nursery just as one of PANCH's paediatricians was putting an IV drip into

Lauren's tiny hand. As he pierced her skin she began to cry. It made me flinch.

'Can I touch her?' I asked, edging nearer.

Lauren was enclosed in an oxygen headbox – a perspex box around the baby's head that ensured the oxygen wouldn't escape when the doors of the isolette were opened. So I could reach into the isolette and place my finger on to her hand. She grabbed it tight and seemed to settle. She was breathing by herself with very little distress. I'd seen babies at this gestation who needed to be ventilated, but Lauren was holding her own. I couldn't help thinking her lungs might have been forced to mature when I'd had the discharge two weeks before – Mother Nature at work again.

'She's so strong,' I smiled to Ian. I was pleased to see that our daughter was still pink and breathing well. I decided I'd seen smaller babies and ones that looked less healthy.

It was now past 1 am and Ian looked as exhausted as I felt. 'There's nothing either of us can do, so you should go home and get some sleep,' I told him. 'I'll stay with Lauren until the NETS [Neonatal Emergency Transport Service] team arrive.'

As a reluctant Ian headed off into the night, I sat gazing at Lauren as she continued to grip my finger. An hour later, I became aware of a huddle of people bustling into the nursery. The NETS team had arrived with a portable isolette, oxygen machine and pumps for intravenous infusions. So much gear for a small baby. After preparing the transport cot, a doctor removed Lauren's headbox and lifted her in quickly in order to minimise any loss of oxygen. She seemed unaffected by the move but with a sinking heart I knew it was time to say goodbye. A neonatal nurse stepped forward and took a Polaroid.

'We'll look after her,' she promised, handing me the photo.

Then all I could do was watch as three strangers wheeled my precious two-and-a-half-hour-old daughter away from me. I might have dealt with the other end of this process, but until then I had no idea quite how heartbreaking it felt to be separated from my baby. I felt completely at a loss and strangely empty as they took her away. My instincts told me she was okay, but I knew all too well that could change.

Totally drained and exhausted, at least I was able to get some sleep but when I woke the next morning I immediately reached for the photo by my bedside. The nurse had captured Lauren with her hand up as though she was waving, but far from making me happy it was agonising to look at. All I wanted was to be with her. As I began to cry quietly, Anne walked into the room.

'How are you feeling?' she asked gently. My face said it all.

'Oh Beth, it's not a bad time,' she said, sitting down next to me. 'Babies at this age often never look back! How did she look?'

'Small but really healthy,' I replied.

'Well, that's a good thing!' she exclaimed. Feeling slightly better, I sniffed and nodded.

'Now what the hell am I going to do without you today?' Anne added, her eyes widening. 'I've got ten new students and no clinical educator!'

She headed off to deal with the new students and I waddled up to the sister's station, feeling very tender from the episiotomy, and asked Rhonda to call the intensive care nursery at the Children's Hospital for me.

'Lauren's doing well,' a nurse reassured me. 'Her condition has remained the same and we're giving her oxygen. Hopefully we can get her down to room air soon.'

'I'll be in later this morning with my husband,' I promised.

When Ian arrived a few hours later, I was itching to go see our baby. Half an hour later we were greeted at the nursery by a smiling doctor. 'Lauren is our prize baby,' he said. 'She's improving by the hour.'

It was the best possible news. I couldn't take my eyes off my formidable daughter as he moved on to the subject of breastmilk. 'We need to get her onto the good stuff,' he said. 'Would you be able to start expressing?'

He didn't have to ask me twice – I was longing to feed my baby. They told me they'd keep her intravenous drip going until I was producing enough milk; then, a few minutes later, the consultant confirmed that Lauren would be weaned to room air at midday. As a healthy prem baby she'd remain in an isolette to maintain her temperature, and would be given a small amount of my expressed breastmilk every two hours, through a tube that went into her stomach via her tiny nostrils.

I was so relieved to hear my daughter was now out of the danger zone, I could have cried with joy.

✳

For the next month, life was on hold as we made the daily commute to the Children's Hospital, taking turns to have precious short cuddles with our daughter.

'She looks a bit like a skinned rabbit,' Dad said in his funny farmer way when my parents arrived to see their new granddaughter.

By now I was breastfeeding Lauren once a day and seemed to spend the rest of the time with a pump attached to my boobs. I knew how much milk Lauren needed every three hours, so I'd aim to express that and a bit more to maintain my supply. I'd seen many women give up as their milk diminished or dried up, but I was determined to breastfeed successfully.

'Is that all you're going to do?' Dad asked one day when he caught me pumping in the kitchen at home. 'When you milk a cow, you keep going back to each teat until there's no more.'

As weird as it was to get this kind of advice from my father, he definitely knew a thing or two about milking. From then on I did it Dad's way and my breastmilk production improved no end. Lauren continued to thrive and when she was a month old she was transferred back to PANCH, where I could easily breastfeed her every morning and evening.

Day by day it was a marvel to see how she was filling out and growing. Her little fingers were getting chubbier; her face too, framing her big eyes. She always had plenty of visitors apart from me and Ian: Anne, Rhonda and Frances would check on her progress regularly. Meanwhile, I knitted and crocheted until I had finished a little pink dress and booties for her. None of the other babies in the special care Unit were in dresses but my colleagues allowed me this small liberty.

Finally, after seven long weeks, we were able to take Lauren home. Now the equivalent of 37 weeks' gestation, she weighed 2630 grams (5 pounds 13) and was deemed healthy and well.

At home, I took her into the nursery and laid her on a cot sheet in her cradle. I put her (on her stomach – this was before the days of the SIDS recommendations) on a soft cuddly lamb's woolskin, covered her with blankets to keep her cosy, and stood back to admire my tiny baby in her huge cradle. It was so wonderful to have her home with us at last, to be able to enjoy her in the place she now belonged.

It's funny, but when I reflect on those first few worrying days of Lauren's life, I think I always knew in my gut that she was going to be okay. Now when a mother tells me she has 'a feeling' about her baby, I always listen. In my experience a mother's instinct is usually right.

Chapter 8
Home delivery

Creeping into my sleeping daughter's bedroom, I ran my hand over her silky soft baby hair, pulled the blanket over her and whispered goodnight.

After nine months of being a full-time mum, I was off to do my first night shift. I had no qualms about leaving Ian in charge, and I knew Lauren would be little trouble to him overnight – she usually slept from 7 pm to 7 am, so it was unlikely she'd even notice my absence. In any case, Lauren was already proving to be a real little Daddy's girl and Ian doted on her, despite turning seven shades of green at the waft of a dirty nappy.

'Toughen up, princess,' I joked when I caught him

recoiling from the smell. 'There's going to be a lot more of those little beauties for you.'

As much as I loved being at home and caring for Lauren, I was excited to be getting back to work, and keen to get straight back into the thick of it. My first patient was a 35-year-old third-time mother whose baby was just as eager to get on with things. Though I quickly called for her GP, within 20 minutes I had caught a beautiful baby girl, and I couldn't get over how tiny she seemed. It had obviously been a long nine months since I had held a newborn. She seemed so fragile compared to Lauren!

Once I'd cleared up and ferried the delighted mother and her new baby to the postnatal ward and written up my notes, I was itching to head home to my own daughter. I found her sitting up in her cradle sucking on her dummy and – just as I'd expected – blissfully unaware that her mother had been gone all night. I fed her and headed to bed.

When I woke up in the middle of the afternoon, the house was suspiciously quiet. Outside, I found Ian washing the car and Lauren naked in a bucket of water. She was babbling happily to her dad, who was pretending to understand each word, and everything seemed to be under control. It seemed that this new arrangement would work perfectly. Lots of my friends' husbands, especially colleagues who did shiftwork, were the primary carers some of the time. That's how we survived financially – this was a time when interest rates were at 17.5 per cent, so we needed every penny we could both earn.

I soon got to know a gaggle of PANCH midwives and nurses who were also juggling family life with part-time work. During the week we'd often get together for morning tea, or meet at the park, enjoying watching our babies crawling around together while the older ones explored the playground. At the ripe old age of 29 I felt I had the best of both worlds: I was earning my own money doing a job I loved, but had enough freedom to spend plenty of time with Lauren. I was still teaching antenatal classes for the CEA (with the techniques I'd used during my own labour, so I knew they worked!) and I'd also branched out and become a member of the local Nursing Mothers' Association.

The group had been founded in Melbourne in 1964 by Mary Paton and five other mothers who were frustrated by the lack of support given by doctors and nurses to breastfeed-ing mothers, and changed its name in 2001 to the Australian Breastfeeding Association. Our local branch met every six weeks to discuss ways to support and advise mothers once they came home from hospital. I enjoyed the raised eyebrows when I imparted Dad's useful, if initially confronting, advice about expressing breastmilk in the same way you'd milk a cow!

I remained passionate about breastfeeding, the most natural and convenient way to feed babies. And having breast-fed a premature baby, I felt well-equipped to encourage other women to do so. I was convinced that the ability to breastfeed effectively was as much to do with one's attitude as anything. Nowadays new mothers get so much conflicting advice, it's hard for women to know what is right for them, and we're a more fragmented society so they are less likely to learn the art from other family members. So I felt it was all the more important to give the right advice and encouragement to help the mothers who came to us to feed successfully, so they would never look back.

Three months after Lauren's first birthday, my doctor confirmed I was carrying a New Year baby! Despite the fact we hadn't planned this pregnancy, Ian and I were thrilled – and chuffed that our daughter would soon have a sibling.

Having twice gone into early labour, I was taking no chances with this pregnancy. This time I'd see an obstetrician from the start and give birth in a hospital with an in-house intensive care nursery. 'There's no way I'm going to be separated from my baby this time,' I told Ian. We discussed our options with Virgil, who agreed to refer me again to Hugh Robinson, the obstetrician and ultrasound specialist at the Royal Women's.

After he'd reviewed my medical history, Hugh said it appeared I might have an incompetent cervix (the cervix is supposed to hold the baby in the uterus, and it is deemed 'incompetent' if it opens too early with the pressure of the growing baby). He recommended a way to overcome the problem: putting a stitch in my cervix. Once it had done its job, it would be removed at 37 weeks.

In the meantime he had concerns about my workload and the risk overdoing things might pose. 'It worries me that you're on your feet a lot of time,' he said. 'I'm not saying wrap yourself in cottonwool, but you need to find a way to take it easy.'

Ian and I discussed our options that night, and he was adamant that my wellbeing and the baby's were the most important thing. So although it felt a little strange to stop working again so soon, I quite happily stood down for the rest of my pregnancy. I would have done anything to avoid the trauma of another scare.

With the stitch in place, I felt more confident, and everything appeared to progress normally. Although we hadn't discussed the new baby with 22-month-old Lauren, it didn't take her long to catch on, and soon she was examining my now-bulging stomach with interest. One evening as I was bathing her she pointed to her own little pot belly. 'Look, Mummy, baby,' she said.

I laughed and called to Ian.

'Show Daddy where the baby is,' I said, and she pointed to her bellybutton and giggled.

As my 37th week of gestation loomed, so did the time to remove the cervical stitch, and then I did begin to feel a little anxious. Hugh had warned me that there was a good chance I'd go into labour as soon as it was taken out, so I arranged for Mum to come and look after Lauren on the day of the procedure.

Four days before the big day, I was sitting, spread-legged, on the floor of the lounge counting out small change when I felt a twinge of pain low down in my belly. Contractions. I remembered the feeling of them all too clearly.

I called Ian. 'Oh no, not tonight,' he sighed, to my disbelief. 'I'm too tired!' Giving him a withering look, I staggered to my feet to call my doctor.

'That stitch needs to come out now,' Hugh said. 'Go straight to hospital. I'll meet you there.'

Oh Lord, we hadn't planned for this. I quickly phoned our neighbour and arranged for her to take Lauren for the night. Once Ian had bundled me into the car, my contractions became much more intense. I gripped my belly with every bump. By the time we'd reached the birth suite, they were coming every five to ten minutes.

A stern-looking woman greeted us – it took me only a moment to see that she was one of those midwives who doesn't think being warm to labouring mothers is part of her job. Trust me to get one of those! She placed my legs in stirrups and Hugh cut and pulled out the stitch.

'Five centimetres dilated,' he confirmed. 'I'll leave you for a bit, but I won't be far away. I think you'll be quick.'

By 12.30 pm the pain was excruciating; much, much worse than Lauren's labour – but then again I was carrying a bigger baby. (At this point, I wasn't sure whether that was a good thing after all!)

Remembering my own antenatal advice about breathing deeply, I fixed my gaze on the light fixture above my head.

'The light is on, the light is on, the light is on,' I repeated, as I tried to breathe through the pain. I felt as though I was in a trance, until I was hit by an overwhelming urge to empty my bowels.

'I need to go to the toilet,' I told the midwife.

'You must stay here,' she replied. 'You're too close. You might have the baby in the toilet.'

'If I can't go to the toilet then I need a bed pan,' I pleaded. This was allowed, but the whole process was deeply humiliating, and I couldn't help feeling acutely embarrassed that the smell remained in the room for a long time. In fact, many women defecated while pushing out the baby and any mess was wiped away without fuss, but now it was happening to me, it was impossible to feel so businesslike about it.

Just when I thought things couldn't get any worse, my contractions surged in intensity, and I found myself moaning and groaning loudly. Although I literally couldn't help myself, I hated losing control like this.

After an hour of this almost unbearable agony, Hugh reappeared. Thirty minutes later he was telling me to push. 'I'm not feeling the urge,' I protested. As far as I was concerned, my body would tell me what I needed to do and when.

'Wait!' I growled as the midwife tried to listen to the baby's heart in the middle of a contraction. Even Ian's hand gently stroking my hair was irritating. How much longer would I have to endure this agony? Finally, about 10 minutes later, the urge to push came with a vengeance. With Lauren I'd felt enormous pressure in my bottom, but this time it was though the front of my vagina was being stretched to my chin, and this ghastly sensation tortured me for what seemed a lifetime.

'The head is out,' Hugh confirmed as the sensation finally, thankfully, subsided. After a blissful minute of rest, I could feel another contraction building. As I surrendered again to the overpowering force, I felt the baby slide from my body. I held my breath, waiting for the telltale sound of crying. At last I was rewarded with the sound of a hearty wail, and the midwife passed me a squirming, bald-headed baby. Another girl! She was blonde, gloriously chubby, nice and pink, active and delightfully wriggly. And she was so big compared to Lauren! I smiled at Ian, who had tears in his eyes.

Apart from a bruise on the back of her head, caused by the pressure of the stitch, Clare – as we named her – was perfect. I spent the next hour basking in the joy of snuggling up to her, hardly able to believe that no one was trying to rush her away from me.

As we settled into each other, I breast-fed her often. Demand feeding was now firmly established as the way to feed newborns, and I was all for it – after all, babies don't wear watches! Lauren had been 'trained' into a set hospital routine by the nurses in the special care nursery by the time I'd got her home. Now it was my turn to do things the way I wanted.

By now Mum had arrived to care for Lauren, and on my daughter's second birthday Mum brought her to the hospital to meet her new little sister. As I watched my firstborn walking down the ward, holding her grandmother's hand, I felt a rush of emotion. She seemed so grown-up – no longer a baby. After a fleeting look at her sister, she scrambled up onto my lap for a cuddle and birthday cake. But the following day she ran onto the ward crying, 'Baby! Baby!' and attempted to scale Clare's cot. From then on she doted on her little sister.

Three months later, I was pacing around the backyard wondering if I would ever know peace again. My youngest daughter cried every afternoon, all afternoon. The crying began around 3 pm and often went on for six hours. I'd tried everything – rocking her, massaging her tummy and attempting, unsuccessfully, to give her a dummy. Lauren had taken bottles from Ian like a dream, but Clare would just roll the teat around her tongue and spit it out with bawls of protest. The only time she stopped crying was on my breast.

This time I'd put her to bed in her cradle in the hope I could muster up the resolve to let her cry it out. But after an agonising 15 minutes I opened the door to hear the 'Waaaa! Waaaa!' wails had increased tenfold and she was purple in the face, arching her back and covered in sweat. As tears streamed down my own face I quickly placed her on my breast until eventually she calmed down.

Our GP thought it could be colic. Even then that was an old-fashioned term. Originally colic had been defined as pockets of wind in a baby's bowel, which made the baby very uncomfortable. There were all sorts of potions available as 'cures' for this, some of which even contained alcohol.

Nowadays, colic tends to be the term used to describe a healthy, well-fed baby who nonetheless suffers bouts of inconsolable crying. At the time, my doctor did prescribe some medicine for Clare, and it did stop the tears temporarily, but it also made her very sleepy and uninterested in feeding, so I took her off it again. Lo and behold, the crying resumed.

I wondered how on earth I could continue to bear hearing her in such terrible and constant distress. But, despite my experience as a midwife and a mother, I was out of options: the only way I could see us carrying on was for me to keep Clare on the breast, doing everything one-handed as Ian helped with dinner and looked after Lauren.

It was one of the most difficult periods I had as a mother, and often I was beside myself with exhaustion and an overwhelming feeling of helplessness. I'd spend ages patting Clare to sleep, only to stand on a squeaky floorboard as I left the room, prompting her to start crying again. Other times I'd hold her over my shoulder until she went quiet and then would carefully back up to the mirror in the bedroom to check if she was asleep. Only then would I attempt to place her in her cradle.

It took months, but eventually Clare developed her own routine, and as we celebrated her first birthday, the incessant crying finally ceased. Ironically, Clare's second daughter did the same thing. Clare put it down to milk allergies – Ian just calls it payback!

✳

The antenatal classes at PANCH were still being run by physiotherapists, but in the spring of 1986 I was pleased to hear that the hospital was finally looking for a midwife to join the service. As I'd hoped, bringing in a midwife to teach the classes would expand the advice given to new mums to include breastfeeding, relaxation techniques for labour and early parenting skills. It was everything Anne, Rhonda and I had hoped for. I immediately applied, and to my delight got the job. Soon I was teaching four days a week while Lauren was at school and Clare at daycare.

Life was good that year: the girls enjoyed a glorious summer chasing around the garden and playing in their paddling pool. Watching them hiding behind trees and building dens made me nostalgic for my own childhood. As a young adult, I'd been so keen to leave behind my old sleepy life, but now I had kids of my own, to my surprise I had started to long for the country and the sort of childhood it could offer our girls.

The idea really started to take root after we took the girls to Cudgewa to spend Easter with Mum and Dad. As usual we had a fabulous time, with the girls cooing over the new farm kittens and Dad saddling up the horse to give them a ride. One of the girls' favourite farm activities was getting the chooks to perform 'band practice'. This involved turning Mum's metal washtub upside down and sprinkling chicken food on the top. We'd all fall about laughing as the chooks frantically pecked at the food, making a real din. While the birds were distracted, Lauren and I would sneak into the pen and carefully place the eggs into an old ice-cream bucket.

After four carefree days it was time to head back to Melbourne. Stopping on our way home to enjoy the magnificent view at Wabba Gap, Ian looked thoughtful. 'Would you like to live back in the country?' he asked me out of the blue. Suddenly we realised we had both been yearning for the same thing.

By the time we'd finished the five-hour journey, we'd decided to put our home on the market, and six months later we sold up, ready to find our dream home in the country.

Of course, this meant that I had to resign from PANCH again. It was sad to have to leave the hospital in which I'd learnt so much. I had benefited from the experience and generosity of my colleagues, many of whom had been inspiring mentors to me, and I had of course learnt so much from sharing the journeys of countless mothers and their babies. But I did feel it was time to move on, and have always felt there is more to life than safely staying put in one place. I also had a sense of restlessness, a need for something new and challenging. Of course, this would lead me further afield in good time; for now, rural Victoria was the ideal place for us to spread our wings with our two girls.

This time we wanted to build our own house on a plot that we'd chosen. After a few months of unsuccessful hunting, it was Dad who found us the perfect location. Good old Dad – as soon as we saw the block of land, 10 kilometres out of Wodonga, we knew it was ideal. It backed onto the Baranduda Ranges and had stunning views towards the Murray River and Albury.

So, a month later, with two children, two cats and all our worldly possessions jam-packed into two cars and a truck, we set off for our new life in the country. As Lauren was seven and Clare five, they were already enrolled in the local primary school. Meanwhile, I had an appointment at Wodonga Maternity Hospital.

Sitting behind her desk and wearing a huge veil, Sister Rickard looking forbidding and old-fashioned for 1988, reminding me of the sisters I'd come across all those years before at Albury Base Hospital and Nagambie. But despite her attire she was friendly and impressed by my experience. She offered me a temporary job working day shifts, and, after proving my worth, I was rewarded with a permanent night-duty position for three nights a week. The money was good on nights, and it was when lots of births seemed to happen. Plus, now the girls were at school, I could sleep while they were in class.

Ian was also making headway. He'd met with a local mechanic to discuss setting up a gas conversion business on his premises. Everything seemed to be falling into place. Working three nights a week meant I could spend quality time not only with both my children but with my parents, now that we lived so much nearer to them. I loved that Mum was always at the end of the phone and willing to help with the girls, and Lauren and Clare adored their grandparents and would spend most of their school holidays at the farm.

After a family Christmas on the farm, on Boxing Day we finally moved into our long-awaited new home.

'Looks like we're true country people now,' I laughed to Ian as we curled up with glasses of wine on the sofa in our fabulous new house.

'And thank goodness for that!' he replied.

✳

I'd been with Susie for almost half an hour when she started wanting to push. Her husband suddenly found himself in a headlock as she clung to him and squeezed down with all her might. Before long, her efforts paid off and her baby came sliding out.

It was just after 1 am when the proud dad kissed his wife and son goodbye and headed home to the family's dairy farm and the couple's two older boys. The rest of the night was uneventful. As dawn broke I returned to the nurses' station after doing my rounds, and discovered my colleague Leanne looking pale and upset.

'The police just called,' she said. 'Susie's husband had a crash on his way home from here.'

'Is he all right?' I asked.

'No,' she said, biting her lip. 'He was dead on arrival.'

My stomach lurched. I'd just come from Susie's room and knew she was awake. Together Leanne and I would have to break the news to her.

I can still hear the terrible, heart-rending shriek she let out when we told her what had happened. I don't know how she carried on but she showed incredible strength over the next few days, rallying to care for her little newborn and her boys.

I often think of Susie: someone who experienced the best and worst moments of her life in one night. At the time, the bitter cruelty of her loss and her extraordinary bravery over the next few days, as she pulled herself together for her little family despite the fact that her heart was breaking, reminded me that life can throw anything at you without warning. We must make the best of our days together.

And it would not be long before I would be reminded of this again.

Just when everything seemed to be happily rolling along in our growing family, Ian and I faced one of the toughest tests of parenthood – our first taste of adolescent rebellion. Up until now the girls had loved staying on the farm during their school holidays. They would come home full of stories of picnics in the paddock with their cousin Andrea, collecting firewood for sausage sizzles, rolling races down the hill and generally running wild. However, this holidays the girls had other ideas.

'We want to stay here,' Lauren announced as Clare looked on sulkily. Oh great, double divas!

While I knew the girls were old enough to be in the house while I slept during the day, I felt guilty and a little nervous about leaving them unsupervised. But perhaps the time had come to allow them to be independent?

'Okay, if this is what you want. Just remember that we're trusting you,' Ian warned. 'You'd better behave while your mother rests.'

As it happened, our girls proved to be very capable, making sandwiches for lunch and entertaining themselves quietly while I slept. But it did make me think twice about working antisocial hours. I put in a request to change to days and soon I was covering morning and evening shifts instead.

But none of us realised that the girls had just missed their last opportunity to spend a holiday with their grandparents on the farm. Less than three months later, Mum was diagnosed with bowel cancer.

I was at work on my 41st birthday when she was admitted to Wodonga Hospital for an operation to remove a small section of malignant tissue. She had been having routine colonoscopies as she'd had a bit of a scare a few years earlier when she'd had to have a malignant polyp removed. Her last colonoscopy had revealed a malignancy in a small section of bowel, which the doctor had told her could be an irritation from the bowel prep.

After a tense day, I met Dad and Faye outside intensive care. 'She'll probably be out of it, and there will be tubes everywhere,' I warned them. In fact, she looked surprisingly good. She was asleep in bed without a tube in her nose and her doctor greeted us warmly. The last thing I expected was bad news.

'The operation took longer than I expected and the cancer has spread. It looks worse than I anticipated,' he began. 'Most of it was outside of the bowel, so Lorraine will likely need chemotherapy.'

As he spoke my mind was racing. Immediately I had a bad feeling that Mum's prognosis was poor. Yet she was only 61, didn't drink alcohol and had never smoked. This should not be happening to her.

As Mum recovered from the operation over the next two weeks, I visited her whenever I could and most days Lauren and Clare would meet me there.

'I made this for you, Granny,' Clare said one afternoon as she handed over a homemade 'Get Well Soon' card. On the front she had drawn a person with a bandaid on her bottom, which made us all laugh.

Mum began chemotherapy: six courses scheduled over six months. Each course took five days, during which she stayed with us. I urged her to call out for help if she needed it, but of course she never did. Instead, I would wake to the sound of vomiting and find her doubled up in bed heaving into a plastic bowl. I knew she hated me seeing her so vulnerable but there was no way I would let her go through it alone. So I'd sit by the bed, mopping her brow with a cool cloth and urging her to take small sips of water. It was a strange role reversal, nursing my fragile mother. How I hated seeing her suffer.

After five months of chemo, Mum was at her wits' end. One of the worst side effects for her was less about the pain and more about her self-esteem. Losing her hair was the final insult: prior to her illness, she'd never left the house without it being perfectly coiffed. Determined to keep up appearances, she rotated a collection of scarves. But there was no escaping how gaunt she looked. Her clothes hung off her and she was tired all the time. I had a terrible feeling of dread. One day I came straight out with it. 'What's going on, Mum?' I asked as we sat drinking tea in the kitchen at the farm.

'I've got a lump on my abdomen,' she admitted. 'The cancer's still spreading. But I'm not having any more chemotherapy.'

'Have you been advised to have chemo?' I asked.

'I've made up my mind. I'm not having any more,' Mum snapped. 'I don't want to hear another word about it.'

That night I closed the door of my bedroom, crumpled onto my bed and cried into my pillow. Mum was losing her battle. Worse, she didn't want to fight it anymore. It broke my heart.

*

Three weeks into 1995, Faye called me at work. 'I think you'd better come,' she said. 'Mum's in hospital in Corryong and she's not good.'

When I got to the hospital, I was shocked to see how much she'd deteriorated in a few weeks. Her eyes were hollow and her face drawn. She wasn't wearing her headscarf and seemed indifferent to the tufts of patchy, grey hair on display. Instead she was agitated about needing the toilet all the time – I think the new growth must have been pressing on her bowel. Whenever she became restless the nurses would administer another morphine injection, so she must have been in intolerable pain. Faye and Dad had been by her side most of the day.

I sent them home to rest and took over. Later, as Mum drifted in and out of sleep, I managed to coax her into having a small amount of soup for her tea. As night rolled in, I settled into the chair beside her bed, jumping to attention every time she stirred or tried to get out of bed to use the commode.

'Help me up,' she called out at 5 am, desperate to get to the commode. I persuaded her to let me give her a shower, hoping that the warm water on her body might make her feel better and help her settle. I asked a night duty nurse to quickly change her sheets, then together we helped Mum back into bed. As the dawn light began to creep under the blinds, I was relieved to watch her slipping into a peaceful sleep. She was still asleep when Dad, Faye and Andrea arrived. This time I went home and put myself to bed, but soon after, I awoke with a start when the phone rang. Faye told me Mum was unconscious and I should come back in.

Back at the hospital I found Mum with a peaceful look on her face and Dad holding her hand. I had just stepped out of the room to put flowers in a vase when Faye rushed out to find me. 'Come back,' she said. 'I think she's going.'

We walked back into the room just as Mum took her last breath. Dad broke down. As Faye and I wept into each other's shoulders, I'm not sure what broke my heart more – losing Mum or seeing Dad so utterly lost and grief-stricken. Like Mum, my father had always contained his emotions – the only other time I'd seen him cry was after his own father died when I was 12.

He was still numb when we held Mum's funeral service a week later. Close to 500 people came to pay their respects but I doubt Dad could even remember who was there. As the guests dwindled and the sun went down, we huddled together, trying to find comfort in talking about our last shared memories of Mum.

However, the brutal truth had hit home – we had no choice but to get on with life without her.

Chapter 9
The circle of life

Eight weeks after Mum's death, Faye rang me, worried about Dad. 'He says he feels confused and can't get his words out. I've taken him to the doctor twice now, but no one knows what's wrong.'

Dad was still living on the farm but he was struggling to cope without Mum. Faye was doing all his cooking and washing, so he was pretty much dependent on her. After 43 years of marriage, he must have been unbearably lonely without Mum but he put on a good show of emotional self-sufficiency. As Faye and Paul were about to head off on a much-needed holiday, I wondered if he was anxious because they were going away. Faye was convinced it was more serious though. In fact, she was so concerned, she ended up postponing their holiday and persuading his doctor to refer him for an ultrasound.

A week or so later I was in the kitchen with my neighbour, Sue, when Faye called again. 'Dad's ultrasound came through while I was at work,' she said. Her voice was shaking and she was barely holding back tears. 'Beth, he's got a brain tumour.'

I listened, dumbstruck, as she explained that the ultrasound had revealed that he had a five centimetre-wide tumour on the left side of his brain. She said it would need to be operated on immediately if there were to be any hope of saving Dad's life.

'He has to be in Melbourne on Monday for the surgery,' she said. 'He went to the races this afternoon so he doesn't know yet.'

I burst into tears and began to cry uncontrollably. I felt guilty for suggesting Dad might have been playing for attention, but mostly I think it was because any mental strength I'd scrabbled together after Mum's death collapsed at that moment. I felt completely broken and battered. I was still deep in grief for my beloved mother, the anchor of our family, and the residual grief of losing Desma had risen to the surface with the loss of Mum. Now this. I could hardly make sense of it. How could this be happening? And how on earth would I keep going without the two people I loved and relied on so much, and who knew me better than anyone?

I was so grateful that Sue was there. As soon as she saw my reaction, she took charge and shepherded Lauren and Clare to another room so I could call Ian. I splashed water on my face, blew my nose and tried to compose myself before I rang him to break the news. He sounded shaken and said he'd come straight home. Once I'd recovered a little, I phoned Faye back to see what I could do to help.

'The doctor's here,' she said. 'We've decided that Dad and I should travel down to your place on Sunday night so we can drive to Melbourne together.'

That night I lay in bed clinging to Ian, unable to sleep. Just getting through each day since Mum's death was a mammoth effort. I felt lost without her. The thought of also losing Dad was too heartbreaking to bear. As far as I knew, brain tumours rarely had a good outcome. I was convinced Dad had been handed a death sentence.

On Monday morning, Faye, Dad and I sat in the kitchen anxiously waiting for the Royal Melbourne Hospital to summon him in for his operation. Our anxiety levels had reached breaking point by 2.30 pm, when we'd still had no word from them. Dad was understandably agitated so I rang the neurological department and they told me to bring him in. The drive was more than three hours, but once we were there he was swiftly admitted to a ward and Faye and I left to spend the night with an old family friend. It made me feel even sadder when I realised that the last time we'd seen her was at Mum's funeral.

At hospital the next morning we were informed that Dad's operation had been scheduled for the following day. His surgeon listed all the possible complications of the surgery, ranging from deterioration of speech and muscle weakness to death. Dad must have been very scared but he didn't let on – and we knew by now he was good at putting on a brave face. 'Don't come in tomorrow,' he told us. 'Take my wallet and go shopping.'

We certainly weren't going to spend a cent of his, but we quietly agreed to take his wallet for safekeeping. After a last hug, as I walked out of the door I tried to give him a reassuring smile. But the truth was, I was absolutely terrified he might not survive the surgery.

We were both restless that night and woke early on Wednesday. We couldn't bear to sit around watching the clock, so we got a tram into the city and walked up and down Bourke Street, killing time. We returned to the hospital when Dad was expected to be out of theatre. A nurse led us to the recovery ward where, to our great relief, we found Dad sitting up in bed. His head was bandaged but he looked surprisingly cheery. 'Well, I'm still here,' he announced with a smile.

Back on the ward, Dad's surgeon explained that he had managed to remove a lot of the tumour and we must now await the pathology results.

A month later the three of us went back down to Melbourne to learn Dad's fate. The neurologist spoke to him first then asked to speak to Faye, as Dad's primary carer. When she returned to the waiting room Dad was in the toilet. She looked wretched.

'The tumour is malignant and aggressive,' she said. 'The doctor says Dad has 18 months at the most to live; he might not make it to Christmas, and he definitely won't be here at Easter.'

Deep down I'd always felt sure Dad's chances weren't good, but to have it confirmed was shattering. I went into denial mode, hardly able to take in the news. There must be some way to prolong his life? Faye said the doctor had suggested radiation therapy. 'He hasn't told Dad the cancer is terminal, and I don't think we should,' she added.

We agreed it was best Dad remained hopeful the treatment could cure him, and indeed after the meeting he seemed sure that the radiation would blast the cancer and he'd soon be better. We certainly didn't want to destroy his optimism, or for him to give up.

Back at home, I knew I had to break the news to the girls that Poppy was very ill. I tried to explain their grandfather's condition without breaking down on them. They didn't like it when I cried, so I'd had to hide a lot of tears from them recently.

'Is Poppy going to die?' Clare asked.

'I don't know, love,' I replied. 'The doctors are doing everything to help him.'

Although this seemed to appease 13-year-old Clare, I was dismayed to see Lauren's face crumpling. 'I don't want Poppy to die,' she said, as tears began to trickle down her cheeks.

'I know, darling,' I said, struggling to keep it together. 'But we have to try to be positive, and do our best to help Poppy feel better.'

Dad's four-month course of radiation therapy began two weeks later. It left him sore and exhausted, and every session drained him a little more. After each course, I'd stay at Faye's to help nurse him while Ian took over running our household, making dinner and ferrying the girls to and from school. He never complained about this, bless him, although I discovered much later that he too was struggling to cope with what was going on in our lives. I was so immersed in helping Dad and trying, still, to get over Mum's death that Ian picked up the slack at home without either of us realising quite how much he was doing. It was like we were both on autopilot, and neither of us talked about the strains we were under.

'That bugger hasn't got me yet,' Dad announced after his last session – feisty old Dad! He was keen to get back to life on the farm and, to our huge relief, despite a tender-looking patch of shaved scalp, he did seem well at this point. The farm had been tended to by my brother-in-law, Paul, while Dad was away, but now the radiotherapy was over, it was good for him to have something else to focus on. He loved his cattle, so checking them each day was a form of therapy for him as he tried to regain some of his strength.

*

That Christmas, the first without Mum, was difficult for us all, but we kept up the façade. We all spent time at Faye's farm, where Dad was now living, and he joined us by the campfire each night to tell stories about his childhood. Dad had been too young to fight in World War 2 but his older brothers had gone into the army so he'd abandoned his dreams of going to teaching college, instead leaving school at 14 to help on the family farm. We made the most of these moments, savouring these special stories of his past and his obvious enjoyment in the telling of them. But underneath it all we were frightened, and it was a strange summer's holiday.

February and March passed. The doctor had predicted that Dad would be dead by Easter, but as April came and went he still seemed well. I started to wonder if the hospital had been overly pessimistic. But then he started to get backache. He was quick to blame it on lifting a heavy chainsaw, but as his pain increased Faye and I began to suspect the worst.

'He's become so grumpy,' my sister told me tearfully over the phone. 'He's always criticising me for not cleaning the dishes, or leaving the eggs out at room temperature. He gets at me for the smallest things.'

In a matter of weeks Dad was bed-bound from the pain. It became a struggle for him to pass water and eventually he was admitted to Corryong Hospital and a catheter was put in to relieve his toileting anxiety.

'That bloody chainsaw,' he told me when I went to visit. 'A bloke would be better if he hadn't lifted it.'

Having been warned that he'd be unlikely to leave hospital now, I tried to have a heart-to-heart with him. 'Is there anything you would like to tell me, Dad, anything at all?' I asked. I wanted to give him the chance to share anything important he might have on his mind. I thought by now he must know he didn't have long.

'Yes, please,' he said. 'I'd like some fish and chips.'

Typical Dad – not one to get sentimental! So off I went in search of the best fish and chips I could find. Dad could only manage a handful of chips and a bite of fish, but it was enough to make him smile.

I was glad I could do something, however small, and even more so when I look back and realise that was our last good day together. In the three weeks that followed he was in so much pain that the only thing to keep him comfortable was morphine, which made him sleepy and disorientated.

Heartbreakingly, Dad's demise was just like Mum's, as he slipped into unconsciousness and out of our lives. I'd thought I'd stay with him until the end, but I found I couldn't bear to listen to him struggle to breathe. He sounded like he was drowning in the fluid in his lungs. I had heard death rattles many times before but, after everything, I couldn't stay and listen to my own father dying.

The call came in the early hours of 5 June 1996, when I was at Faye's. We hugged for a long time then made tea.

I sat at the table staring into space, unable to cry, unable to do anything. Our father had died at the age of 66, less than 18 months after we had lost Mum. I was 43 years old, but I felt like a frightened, bewildered orphan.

✳

The funeral, and being able to celebrate Dad's life, kept Faye and me afloat in the immediate aftermath of Dad's death. As I knew from losing Mum, it was the next period that was the hardest. Life ground on but we carried the burden of a terrible aching loss, more painful than ever now neither of our parents were with us. Not only that, but Faye and I had the emotional task of dividing the assets of the farm on which we had grown up.

Faye and Paul kept her percentage of the land to expand their Black Angus stud farm and I sold the 300 acres of land bequeathed to me. Farewelling the land and house where our family had spent so many years was yet one more loss on top of too many others. I really did feel as though I had lost my way. I almost couldn't make sense of who I was for a while – losing my parents and our home made me feel as though great big chunks of my past had been wiped out.

When Ian, the kids and I had moved back to the country, I'd envisaged many years with my parents, sharing the joys of watching our children and their grandchildren growing up. I had imagined celebrating their landmark birthdays as they navigated their 70s and hopefully their 80s. The feeling of emptiness now they'd gone was indescribable, and my grief seemed bottomless.

I tried to immerse myself in work, but for a long time just turning up for my shifts and going through the motions was all the effort I could conjure up. Having experienced two unrelenting years of worry, illness and grief, I think I had forgotten how to be happy.

One night I was drifting off to sleep when I realised that Ian was crying quietly next to me. I jolted awake, wondering what could have upset him so much, and was astonished when he falteringly told me that he felt I didn't need him anymore. I was devastated. Poor Ian. Suddenly I realised how much I'd been shutting him out – of my grief and my life – since Mum and Dad had died. I'd immersed myself in my parents' deaths – dealing with the undertakers, organising the funerals, going to the solicitors, selling the farm – and all the time he'd felt cut off and starved of love and affection.

I threw my arms around him and told him how much I loved and needed him. It made me realise how the pain of grief can make us neglect the ones we love. We vowed not to take each other for granted ever again – no matter how bad things were, or how long we'd been married.

It was probably this realisation that led Ian and I to get away from it all and take the girls on a four-wheel-drive tour across the country from our home in Victoria to the Northern Territory. It was something we'd often talked about in the past and now seemed exactly the right time. So we headed up north in September 1996, stopping along the way wherever we wanted to explore, until we reached Big Red, a huge sand dune just outside Birdsville in Queensland, more than 1500 kilometres west of Brisbane. It was stunning: the landscape seemed to change after every dune we crossed, like a kaleido-scope of postcards. It had rained recently, too, so the ground was covered in wildflowers – carpets of purple, yellow and white.

Our convoy continued through the Simpson Desert, east to Witjira National Park, right at the top of South Australia on the border with the Northern Territory. From there we headed to Uluru, where we set up camp and awaited the sunset. With the sunlight fading into the western sky, we watched, awestruck, as the rock appeared to turn on a light-show of its own, transforming from a rusty-red to a velvety mauve, until it finally faded to black. I cuddled up to Ian, feeling as though at last I might be able to see some light in my life again.

There was a final high point on our journey home. We visited the Aputula Aboriginal community, a remote settle-ment nearly 160 kilometres south of Alice Springs. Our convoy attracted a lot of interest from a crowd of inquisitive Aboriginal children and in turn I found myself drawn to them. There was something about the place and the people we met there. It was as though they lodged in my head, got to me. As we left, I wondered if I could live and work somewhere like this. Would I be up to it?

'Can you imagine if I got a nursing job in a place like this?' I said to Ian. 'We'd get the full experience of living remote. And I could get back to doing what I love most about being a midwife.'

As we passed signs for other Aboriginal communities, all of which you needed a permit to visit – just as you'd need permission to go on to anyone's land – I continued to wonder about life for the people who lived up here. What access did they have to medical care? How did they deliver their babies? Could this be somewhere I could get back to the real basics and joys of being a midwife, using *all* of my skills and experience where they were needed most, and dealing directly day to day with mothers and their babies, without having to defer to anyone else?

With those thoughts and all the possibilities they presented in the back of my mind, I was beginning to feel alive again, to feel more hopeful about the future and what it might hold.

When we got back to Wodonga, I also felt quietly optimistic that after four years of family turmoil, we could get to the end of year without any more upset.

But in December, I was summoned to Clare's school by her teacher. To my absolute horror and amazement, she told me that Clare hadn't been attending school for most of the second half of the year, and she'd therefore failed Year 9.

I was shocked, and livid – both with the school and Clare. Why hadn't they warned me earlier that Clare had been wagging? How could Clare have deceived me like this, or had I missed obvious signs in my grief about Mum and Dad? Had Ian and I failed her somehow, or was she just being a selfish, stupid teenager? I didn't know what to think as I left the meeting, my head spinning.

I frogmarched my wayward daughter to the car and confronted her as she slumped into the passenger seat. It turned out that for the past two terms Clare had been getting on and off the bus to school at the right time, but in between had been hanging around with various people, including an exchange student who was staying with us, with whom she'd become great mates. She was sheepish, though she didn't offer me an apology. But it was hard not to blame myself as well. No doubt my attention had been elsewhere, and she'd taken advantage of that, as teenagers can do.

After a stressful few days, and with Ian's agreement, we decided she shouldn't return to the school, and instead secured a Year 10 place for her at a local private school. The fees were expensive but we felt it was crucial to get her back under some proper supervision, and a few girls there had been with her at primary school so it wouldn't be a completely alien environment.

'Don't let us down,' Ian warned. 'You'll only let yourself down if you do.'

At the same time as this was going on, Lauren was off to Norway for a year as an exchange student. In July 1997, shortly before her 17th birthday, Ian and I saw her off at the airport. It was hard to let her go, but I tried to be brave about it. Hadn't I wanted to escape the country as a teenager? Now I had to let my daughter spread her wings too.

Halfway through the next school year, it became clear that Clare was struggling to settle into her new school. She told me she hated it there, and Ian and I struggled with how much to push her. It was a terribly hard decision, but there was no pleasure in seeing her miserable and perhaps as unproductive as she'd been the previous year, so eventually we agreed she could return to Wodonga High School.

But even back there, Clare simply couldn't make herself study, and by the end of the year she had moved out of home. All she would tell us was that she was 'staying with friends in Wodonga'. No amount of talking could get through to her and we came to the reluctant realisation that our headstrong 17-year-old would have to learn from her own mistakes.

While I tried – and failed – not to worry about her, a few weeks later Clare turned up unexpectedly at Ian's workshop. 'I think I need discipline in my life,' she announced. 'I want to join the military and train to be a cook.'

This sudden about turn completely blindsided us. She'd never appeared to listen to what we had to say, so I found it difficult to believe she'd be happy to be told what to do by lots of other people! All we could do, though, was support her decision and sit back and see what came of it.

Ian helped her to set up interviews and before long Clare had secured a post in the RAAF and was off to begin her 10-week recruit training in Adelaide. After that she was posted to the naval college at HMAS *Cerberus* on the south coast of Victoria, where she learnt to be a cook. We were so proud of her when she made it through recruit training – 10 weeks of intense physical and mental rearrangement!

Although Clare's military career was short, she subsequently set up a successful cake decorating business, of which she is justly very proud.

Shortly after Clare made her decision to go into the air force, Lauren returned from Norway and found a job as a travel agent in Melbourne.

Ian and I were now bona fide empty nesters!

❉

Over the next two years, the closest hospitals to Wodonga, Albury Base and Mercy, lost their maternity units, widening our catchment from a population of between 35,000 and 45,000 people to about 100,000. Wodonga became the centre for midwifery services in the region and our birth tally suddenly doubled to 1600 a year. We were in dire need of upgraded facilities.

Finally, at the beginning of 2000, a maternity wing funded by the Victorian government opened at Wodonga, with six plush birthing rooms. Fortunately it had been built at the other end of the hospital so we were able to continue to work in the old unit until the flash new one was finished.

When we saw the unit, I couldn't help be impressed by the lengths the architects and designers had gone to, to ensure it was homely and welcoming. The rooms had all the mod cons – even a television suspended from each ceiling. Intimidating equipment such as IV poles, oxygen and suction equipment was hidden away behind cupboard doors. A larger room contained a double birthing bed for low-risk, straightforward births, and we had access to birthing balls and a lovely deep spa bath for pain relief. The wing imme-diately reminded me of the home-birth environment I'd so loved at the Royal Women's Hospital when I'd set eyes on it twenty years before.

With plenty of time on my hands, and this wonderful new environment to work in, I happily increased my shifts at the hospital to four days a week. At first, getting back into the thick of things and daily life on the ward was great, the work just as varied and fulfilling as I'd hoped. It was wonderful to see women in labour moving around freely and enjoying the benefits of being able to submerge themselves in the warm, bubbling waters of the spa bath to help with their pain. All the women in our care loved the comfy new suites and felt supported and empowered by all the options they had for giving birth.

But then word began to circulate that one of the obstetric doctors had made a formal health and safety complaint about the double birthing bed. According to this GP, the bed was a 'safety hazard' because it could obstruct his access to a patient's airway in an emergency situation. His other gripe was that he 'might' have to lean further across the bed and therefore risk a back injury. He really had a bee in his bonnet and was determined to have something done about it. And in the end he got his way. His protests led to a health and safety evaluation, and to everyone's bitter disappointment the bed was given its marching orders.

No doubt spurred on by his victory, the doctor put in his next complaint – this time about the 'perilous' spa bath that labouring women so loved for pain relief. Another investigation ensued and within months it too had been deemed unsafe – for staff, of course; never mind about the women in labour for whom it was intended – unless a lifting device was attached to the roof to haul out any woman who might collapse in it. Of course, the cost of installing such a device was beyond anyone's budget, so our beloved spa was covered up and the space became a storeroom.

While so many hospitals were moving forwards with midwifery-led models of care, we had taken what had looked like such an exciting step forward, just to go backwards again. It was not only very frustrating for the mothers in our care but a major blow to staff morale.

After all my hopes of exploring new frontiers in my work, I was bitterly disappointed with the way Wodonga maternity care was being stifled. Still reeling from the terrible personal toll of the preceding years, I began to feel increasingly unmotivated and downright despondent about my job.

Determined to try to improve my situation, I took a senior position on the birth suite overseeing weekends, nights and evening shifts, but although it was a challenge for a while, I was soon bored. When Wodonga began a student midwife teaching program, I duly threw myself into that. But yet again I found myself dogged by a need to shake things up in my life. As my fifties passed me by, month by month, it felt as though life was moving on but, with nothing to inspire me, I was staying still, stagnating.

I tried various ways to cure this sense of inertia. Ian and I took on house renovation projects, made trips to Sydney when our daughters moved to the east coast and took more road trips to the outback. It was during one such holiday that I decided to call on Dianne, an old friend from my days at PANCH.

Although I hadn't seen Dianne since Ian and I had left Melbourne 18 years before, I'd heard on the grapevine she was working as a remote area nurse, managing a clinic in Jabiru, a Northern Territory mining and tourist town in Kakadu National Park, and I was eager to hear all about it.

Dianne was delighted to see us and that night we met her and her husband, Dave, for dinner. I have to admit I spent most of the evening grilling her about her work. The idea of working somewhere remote where I felt both Ian and I could share our skills and perhaps actually make a difference had been brewing away in my mind for some time now and I wanted to know what it was like working as a midwife there, compared to in a busy, urban hospital with all the latest technology.

It was immediately clear that Dianne loved working at Jabiru, and her enthusiasm for her job there, and in other remote communities, was infectious. She felt valued for her knowledge, and she was also supported with opportunities to explore new areas or expand on her skills. Both Dianne and Dave enjoyed the relaxed lifestyle, even if they were forever on high alert for emergency call-outs, such as helicopter rescues of walkers in the national park or car accidents involving multiple casualties. Dave would sometimes assist by driving the ambulance, and also at the accident sites. Ian loved the idea of this – he could really see himself there, he told me afterwards. As we talked I felt a tingle of excitement – something I hadn't felt for ages.

'You should consider it,' Dianne smiled. 'I think you'd be great.'

After dinner, I boldly told Ian I'd like to start applying for work in the outback, rather than just talking about doing it one day. I'd wondered if he'd protest, but he nodded. It was as though, hearing Dianne's story, something had clicked for us. Also, Ian knew me well enough to know I had to do this or I'd always wonder. As for taking such a big leap, after the last few years, I didn't feel anxious or frightened about uprooting myself from my home and everything I knew. The losses I'd suffered made me realise there is no point just thinking and dreaming about doing things. You had to make them happen.

I also had to factor in how I felt about what was going on at the hospital. During the past year or so, the College of Midwives had developed Guidelines for Consultation and Referral, to empower us to provide the safest possible practises in our workplace. At the same time the Victorian government was developing midwife-driven programs for hospitals. It seemed exactly the right time for us to change the way we worked in the maternity unit at Wodonga, so I wrote a letter to the management of the hospital suggesting we grasp this chance for development, now there was so much assistance available to instigate and support a different way of delivering maternity care.

The result was that I began working on a project funded by the Victorian government to look at increasing midwifery models of antenatal care at the hospital.

However, despite all my efforts and those of fellow midwives and our supporters, it soon became clear that the obstetricians were calling the shots and had the ear of the decision-makers at the hospital, whereas we as midwives did not. We felt as though our credibility was being completely undermined.

Essentially, the obstetricians wouldn't support any extra midwifery-led care. One told me directly that their livelihood was on the line. I reminded them that they were valued for their work with high-risk patients and complicated births, and that midwives could help reduce the crisis of ageing obstetric doctors that would soon hit the hospital. But it seemed to fall on deaf ears. So my frustration with this brick-wall mentality was another motivating factor pushing me to look outside the square when it came to new jobs.

As soon as we got home, I contacted an agency that I'd been told might be able to offer me work out of the city. At the same time I made quiet enquiries about the possibility of taking a leave of absence from Wodonga for a few months. I knew I needed to keep my options open so I didn't want to hand in my notice immediately. Our human resources department seemed open to the idea.

A few months later the agency offered me a phone inter-view. My interviewer said I needed more emergency nursing experience, but before I could feel disheartened she went on,

'We have vacant positions at Kununurra or Derby Emergency Department that might help you. Once you get there, they'll probably take you into midwifery.'

I didn't waste time. 'I'll go to Derby,' I replied – recalling that a friend I'd worked with in Wodonga had spent a year there a year and loved it.

Talk about an on-the-spot decision! And a life-changing one.

Chapter 10
Bush-bound

Walking up the steps to the plane, I blinked away tears and took a last look at Ian, who stood smiling through the window of the terminal. We'd been married for 35 years but we'd never spent more than a couple of weeks apart before. Suddenly I felt a little off-balance, about to face a major new challenge alone, without my number one supporter and best friend at my side. While we'd agreed it made more sense for Ian to stay at home to oversee the final stage of renovations to our house while I headed off to Western Australia, I couldn't help regretting it now.

I told myself not to be silly, to pull myself together, but by the time I got to my seat tears were streaming down my cheeks. I had to remind myself how lucky I was to be taking six months' leave from my job. After months of wishing, hoping and dreaming of doing something radically different and putting all my years of experience to work in a challenging new environment, I was off to pursue my dream job. It was time to put aside my fears and look forward to the next chapter of my life!

Four and a half hours later – and feeling a lot more composed – I stepped off the plane in Broome, to be greeted by blazing sunshine and a wall of dry heat, fanned by a warm wind. I found the bus station, grabbed a cup of tea and an hour or so later boarded the coach that would take me 220 kilometres north-east to Derby in the heart of the Kimberley.

It was an unforgettable journey. My mind was racing as I took in every glimpse of scenery rushing by my window along the way – red, rocky outcrops and scrubby bush dotted with tall savannah grass, and an endless blue sky. As dusk fell, the driver explained that he was slowing down to keep an eye out for any sudden appearance on the bush-lined roads of wild Brahman cattle and kangaroos, notorious for causing major accidents on this stretch of road. But fortunately for us that night the road was quiet, apart from a 'whooooosh' when a long road train passed us.

Soon I began to spot boab trees – the alien-looking, bottle-shaped trees with a thick trunk at the bottom and thin, spindly branches sprouting out in a canopy from the top. I knew they were unique to the Kimberley and I felt a rush of adrenalin at the thought of being so far from home and so near my destination.

Having studied up on my new home, I had become even more fascinated about the culture of the Kimberley: apparently there were 27 language groups in the region! It was of course home to some amazing rock art and even bark paintings, which I was hoping to have time to see. Derby had been the first white settlement in the Kimberley. It was built on an ancient sand dune on the King George Sound, and was known as the 'western gateway' to the Windjana Gorge and Tunnel Creek National Parks. I couldn't wait to look around and get to know the place.

The first thing I noticed as we arrived in Derby were the town's extraordinarily wide streets, built that way so mule or camel teams could turn in them in the first days of settlement. Although I was exhausted, I felt a thrill as we pulled into the tourist information centre. Warren, an orderly from the hospital, was waiting to welcome me, and drive me to my new home. My escort's car was a Derby hospital ambulance – when it wasn't being used for emergency call-outs and transfers to the Royal Flying Doctor Service (RFDS) base, it doubled up as a people mover.

Warren took me just a couple of blocks to a small cement building – my new home. I opened the door to a tired-looking unit, and was immediately assaulted by a powerful, musty smell. Inside were two sad-looking green fabric chairs that looked as though they'd escaped from the 1960s, and a small laminated coffee table. The bedroom had a double bed with a skinny mattress and electrical wires hanging out of the wall where a light should have been. The bathroom (and laundry) had a shower, a basin and scruffy-looking cupboards with peeling laminate where the timber had swollen. Peering into the toilet bowl, I jumped as I spotted a luminous green frog eyeballing me, looking affronted at having his peace and privacy disturbed.

I hadn't been expecting the Taj Mahal, but after all my anticipation I felt a bit deflated at how basic my accommodation was. I quickly shook myself. Come on – you're not a princess. You don't need everything to be grand; you have what you need so get over yourself. I carefully scooped up the frog and deposited him outside.

Tiredness was washing over me, so rather than let it all overwhelm me, I thought the best thing to do was get some sleep. It would seem better in the morning. I made up the bed with the old, bobbly sheets provided, sunk down into the mattress, sighing at the lack of padding or the usual welcome sensation of springs, and was out like a light within minutes.

The next morning I woke early, still on Melbourne time, and took a stroll down to the jetty for my first sight of the magnificent swirling waters of the King George Sound. I had read that Derby has some of the largest tidal movements in the world and this was proof positive. Because of these huge tides, which can vary by 11 metres from high to low, the mud is forever being stirred up, so the water's not clear, as you might expect, but a muddy brown. At low tide, there's nothing but glistening mudflats, and at high tide the Sound transforms – watching it stir to life with the rush of water is mesmerising.

As I strolled around the town, which I pretty much had to myself this early in the day, I was surprised to see how green the parks and gardens were, with sprinklers spreading water in abundance. In Victoria, sprinklers were banned due to the prolonged drought conditions, and I'd expected Derby to be far more barren, dusty with red dirt; instead the town looked clean, lush and sparkling, at the end of the wet season.

My explorations finally led me to the hospital – a modern-looking building with a swish glass atrium. It had been built 18 months before, and it was clear no expense had been spared. The main entrance and corridors were all lined with beautiful Aboriginal art and there was a reassuringly calm vibe to the place.

After breakfast at my unit, I couldn't help feeling a little apprehensive as I prepared for my first day. Arriving back at the hospital, I was told that I would indeed be working in the maternity department, and I was introduced to Caroline, a friendly woman in her early 40s who was a flight nurse for the Royal Flying Doctor Service. She gave me a tour of the maternity ward. I was impressed by the facilities: the two birthing suites had modern electronic beds, and the intravenous and surgical equipment was similar to what I'd used in Victoria. It all seemed very state-of-the-art and I felt at home there, and reassured. I might be a stranger in town but the maternity ward was one place I always knew I belonged.

❋

My first Kimberley baby arrived two days later. Josie, a shy young Aboriginal woman, had been flown in a week earlier from her remote community. As many of these communities have no medics or midwives, just a visiting service, their pregnant women have to spend their last month in Derby to ensure they give birth in a town with the necessary facilities. During that time – known as a 'sit-down' – they'd stay in a local hostel provided by the state government, and this was where Josie had been until her waters broke.

By the time I arrived at work, Josie was well on her way in established labour and her contractions were getting stronger. I found her in the bathroom, crouched on the floor under the shower, using the hot water as pain relief. She was agitated, moving from a squatting position to standing and making groaning noises that made me think she wanted to push.

Gently drying her off, I encouraged her into the birthing suite, where she gripped the side of the bed.

'Get it out, get it out!' she screamed, crouching into a semi-squatting position.

I called for a nurse to assist and positioned myself behind Josie, ready to catch her baby. I could see the dark curls of the top of the baby's head and in next to no time there was a plump little girl in my hands. As Josie's pants of exhaustion slowed, we helped her on to the bed to deliver the placenta. I wiped the baby clean, admiring her big brown eyes and chubby cheeks. I could hardly contain my smile. My first outback delivery – and what a beauty!

When I handed the baby to Josie, she carefully studied her face and her tiny fingers and toes. 'She looks just like my little boy,' she smiled as she placed her to her breast.

'What's her name?' I asked.

'Garrianne,' she said proudly. 'Her dad is called Gary.'

In time, I discovered that it's common practice for Aboriginal mothers to name their babies after the father, whether they're girls or boys. Straightforward enough, then, for the sons to take their dad's name, but girls' names would be adapted accordingly – for example, Owen becomes Owena.

'This is the first time I've delivered an Aboriginal baby,' I told her.

Josie smiled at me and seemed very proud, offering me baby Garrianne for a cuddle and a photo.

That night Caroline invited me to dinner, and filled me in on Derby life over a bottle of wine and some delicious fresh barramundi. She explained that Derby was the referral centre for obstetrics and paediatrics for the whole of the Kimberley region. All high-risk cases were sent to us to be evaluated, and if we were unable to deal with them they'd be referred on to Perth, more than 2000 kilometres away. 'Sometimes we fly six hundred kilometres to get a mother,' she said.

While I understood the reasoning behind it all, I thought the women must find it hard being away from home at such a crucial time. I certainly wouldn't want to spend a month in a hostel before my baby's birth. Caroline agreed and admitted that there were problems with the hostel system, which had been instigated some thirty years back to address concerns about the high rate of infant deaths. It was very basic accommodation, and many of the women felt vulnerable while they were there. They were sometimes 'humbugged', as it was known, by family members wanting money – for food, alcohol, phone cards, you name it.

But, as Caroline pointed out, the evidence was clear that bringing in the women for this time was important, and the reasoning behind it was to enable women to have better access to and equality of care. With nothing but basic or no medical facilities in remote communities, it was much safer for women to give birth in a properly equipped hospital such as the one in Derby, especially when, statistically, babies born to Aboriginal mothers are twice as likely to be born prematurely as those born to non-Aboriginal mothers.

For the next few weeks, my crash-course in local Aboriginal culture continued. Traditionally, in the past, Aboriginal mothers gave birth 'on country', with other women around them and important ceremonies to welcome the child into the world, so there was no doubt that having their baby in a hospital in Derby – as insisted by their health authority – might be a big contrast to their Aboriginal communities, to say the least. While many of the women giving birth in

Derby had also been born there, or in a hospital somewhere in Western Australia, most were eager for their babies to form a spiritual link to the land and were understandably anxious to get back home as quickly as they could.

Occasionally, on a quiet day, I'd be lucky enough to have a woman in my care share a little more about her heritage as we chatted, adding to my education along the way. 'My child will be a future elder for their country,' one young mother, Tahnee, told me proudly. 'He is the first son of his generation on both sides of my family.'

I asked her to explain the significance of some of the laws and lore in Aboriginal culture.

'Men and women have different things to learn,' she said. 'When my son is ten, he will start to go to ceremonies to learn about his country, and the elders will pass on all the knowledge he needs to become a man in the community. If I have a daughter, she will take part in ceremonies that are just for young women. It is very important.'

Of course, I knew Aboriginal communities would have their own dialect and languages, but I'd naively assumed the mothers in my care would be bilingual. I soon discovered that many struggled with English, and whenever my antenatal questioning hit a brick wall, I learnt to call upon Annie, the hospital's Aboriginal liaison worker. From what I could see, Annie worked flat out, with a never-ending list of responsibilities that ranged from translating and assisting with paperwork to register births, to going to Centrelink to organise parenting payments due to some of these new mums.

There was so much to learn it was almost overwhelming. And the most important things I had to learn could not be garnered from books or reports. One day I asked a woman how she'd got so many scars on her leg. She explained to me they were 'sorry' wounds – how she'd cut herself with a machete when her brother had passed away. I'd heard of these practices and should have been prepared for them, but it was one thing to know about them, another to be confronted with their actual results.

There were other things I had to get used to. When I asked an Aboriginal mother when she'd last fed her baby, she looked at me blankly.

'Was it ten, twenty or thirty minutes ago?' I enquired, not sure why she looked so uncomfortable.

'I can't tell the time,' she eventually muttered. Like many Aboriginal mothers, she'd grown up without clocks or watches. I felt bad that I'd been so insensitive but of course it hadn't occurred to me. It was not the first time – nor would it be the last – that I tripped up over things like this. I just had to chalk down to experience, and try to learn as much as I could day by day about the different ways we lived and saw the world.

At first I was concerned that if some mothers had no concept of time their babies might become undernourished. But I began to relax when I saw how their babies were kept on the breast far more than I'd seen before, which also meant milk problems and mastitis, a painful inflammation of the breast, were rare. Generations of mothers and babies had of course survived very well without watching a clock.

Most mothers in Derby Hospital slept alongside their babies, and many were smokers. Of course, they weren't allowed to smoke in the hospital, so they were encouraged to put their baby in the cot before they went outside. But many times they'd leave the baby on the bed, which always frightened me a bit, even if he or she were swaddled.

Smoking as a mother and co-sleeping were against all SIDS (Sudden Infant Death Syndrome) recommendations, but I soon realised I just had to do my best to explain why certain things weren't a good idea. I sometimes had a breakthrough, but it was hard not to worry that once a mother was out of the hospital, it was highly likely my advice would be ignored.

'You're doing so well, Becky,' I assured my young charge, gently mopping away the beads of perspiration and placing a cool cloth on her forehead. The girl, barely 14, was lying quietly on her side, her breathing becoming a little more audible as a contraction washed over her. If she heard me, she didn't acknowledge it. She remained unusually silent, staring into space and enduring each contraction with a steely determination.

A month into my new job, Becky was my youngest patient yet. Throughout her six-hour labour, my colleague, Lisa, and I fussed over her, trying to help and make her as comfortable as we could. It was impossible not to feel sympathy for this brave little girl who was barely out of childhood herself. She was heartbreakingly stoic. It was not unusual for a woman in labour to turn the air blue, but as Becky approached the final stages, she began to express her pain altogether differently.

'In Jesus' name! In Jesus' name!' she called out in soft prayer, her eyes fixed to the wall and the occasional tear escaping down her cheek.

'Becky comes from a community that used to be run by a mission,' Lisa explained later. 'Mothers from there often call out in prayer as they give birth.'

As her baby's head began to crown, Becky let out a groan of a final push, there was a gush of amniotic fluid and her baby slipped into my hands. Blinking in the light of the ward, the little fellow gave a lusty cry and I placed him on his mother's chest as she lay panting.

'It's a boy,' I told her, but her face was blank. I wondered, not for the first time, what circumstances had led to her falling pregnant so young.

'Can you help me dry him off?' Lisa asked her, wrapping a soft, warm towel around the tiny baby. As Becky patted and rubbed softly to wipe off the remnants of his birth, I was pleased to see her now looking more tenderly at the cute little chap. 'My boy,' she whispered, touching his cheek.

As Lisa listened to the little boy's heart and assessed his general condition, I quickly cut the cord, gave Becky the once-over and delivered the placenta. Her baby was in good health so he remained on Becky's chest and it wasn't long before he was searching with his mouth for her nipple. To my relief, she seemed happy to nurse him.

'What will you call him?' I asked as we started cleaning up and putting equipment away.

'Edward,' she replied. 'It's the name my grandfather chose for him.' A small smile escaped her lips.

The next morning, I was pleased to see Becky lying in bed, staring intently at her baby son. The look on her face was one of unbridled love so I let them be and busied myself with the day-to-day chores of the postnatal ward: five new mothers needed to be checked and newborn screening tests had to be done on their babies.

I was just preparing to teach Becky how to bathe her son when two women arrived at the nurses' station. They looked dishevelled. One of them was visibly drunk. 'Where's me daughter?' she slurred loudly.

'Who are you here for?' I asked.

'We've come to see Becky,' the other woman said more quietly. 'I'm her aunt. This is a bit of a shame job,' she said, dropping her eyes. My heart sank. Teenage pregnancies were common in remote communities, but they were often frowned upon. Still, I'd hoped Becky would get encouragement rather than disapproval from her family.

'The baby's doing well,' I offered, trying to keep everything upbeat. 'And Becky's doing a great job.' But when I took them onto the ward, Becky shrunk into her bed.

'So this is ya bub, is it?' her mother asked as she peered, unsmiling, at her new grandchild. By now Becky looked every bit her age. She hugged her knees to her chest and refused to meet her mother's eye.

'You know I won't be able to look after another baby, don't ya,' her mother continued. 'I got enough to deal with meself.'

Becky didn't say a word, keeping her eyes low. You could have cut the atmosphere with a knife.

'Can't stay,' her mother eventually announced. 'Got to go to the office.'

And with that, they left to find what I could only assume was the welfare office.

Two days later, satisfied that Becky was coping well with Edward, I began to prepare their return to her community. They would go home by bus, travelling late into the night – Fitzroy Crossing, the stop nearest to the community, had a midnight arrival. While it was not a bad journey, especially compared to the one the Halls Creek mothers had to do – their bus got in at 4 am – it seemed like a lot for a teenage mum with a tiny baby to cope with. The bus left Derby at 9 pm so I got on with setting up Becky with plenty of blankets, nappies, baby wipes and water for the journey.

But Becky didn't leave that night. Although a second ticket had been provided for her mother to escort her on the bus trip home, she didn't turn up. So a miserable-looking Becky was brought back to the hospital for another night and after several calls to Jill, the Fitzroy midwife, we decided the young girl and her baby would have to travel alone a few days later.

'Mum's off long-grassing, is she?' Jill sighed, referring to how less than reliable relatives sometimes disappeared to get drunk and ended up in the long grass. She agreed to find someone else to meet Becky off the bus and it was with a heavy heart that I discharged the young mother once more later that week.

I was used to sending a mother and baby home to ongoing support from family and a midwife who would make house calls. It made me shudder to think that I was sending out this young girl unsupported, back to a place that didn't sound as though it would be great for her or her baby.

The only thing that gave me any peace of mind was that the Department of Child Protection was involved, and Becky was on their radar. But deep down I felt helpless. I just had to hope there were other more understanding family members in her community, who would take her on board and support her and Edward.

My next challenge in Derby was a 19-year-old girl called Keeley. Keeley had been admitted to hospital a week earlier, at 34 weeks, when her community midwife had become concerned about the diminutive size of her baby bump. We'd been keeping a close eye on her progress, but as I toured the ward one evening I realised she was nowhere to be found. After an hour of calling round trying to locate her, I was relieved to see her coming through the maternity ward doors.

'Have you been drinking?' I asked as I caught a waft of alcohol on her breath.

'I only had six cans!' she said defensively. I put her to bed – there was no point scaring her with talk about foetal alcohol spectrum disorder (FASD) when she wouldn't be able to take it in. The next day I took her aside for a quiet word. 'You know, drinking when pregnant is not a good idea,' I said. 'The more you drink, the more damage you can cause to your baby.'

She didn't say anything and I didn't push it. I'd been told by other, longer-serving staff that if a baby was born with something wrong, I could get the blame – and payback apparently could take many forms, from having your car windows smashed to a spear through the leg. I had come here with an open mind and I knew I had a lot to learn but I was determined not to let things like this interfere with my work. That said, I have to admit that I felt especially relieved when Keeley gave birth three weeks later to a small but healthy baby girl. Having expressed concern about her, I was assured that her child's milestones would be documented for her first several years, and Keeley would be kept under the watchful eye of the Department for Child Protection to make sure her drinking wasn't compromising her ability to mother.

✶

After three long months without my husband, Ian finally motored into town in August, having driven all the way from Wodonga, with Faye to keep him company. What he'd planned as an eight-day trip took him just five as he was so eager to get to Derby – and me. When I heard the familiar sound of his cow horn out the front my heart leapt and I belted out to hug him. It was fantastic to see him grinning from ear to ear. 'We made it in record time,' he announced. 'Only got lost once!'

Shortly after Ian arrived and had settled in, I volunteered to accompany the clinic nurse from Derby on a Royal Flying Doctor trip to Djugerari, a remote community outstation in the shire of Derby-West Kimberley, which consisted of just 20 houses, a community clinic and a primary school. It was about 100 kilometres from Fitzroy Crossing by road. We picked up a doctor en route before beginning our descent between a collection of boulder-strewn hills and landing on a dusty red-dirt runway. We were greeted by a waiting Troopie, the Toyota Troop Carrier used in these remote settlements, to transfer us to the community clinic.

A gaggle of outstation residents were already lining up. My first patient of the day was an elderly Aboriginal stockman. Before he came into the examination room he courteously removed his large Akubra hat and proceeded to tell me how he used to drive cattle into Derby, crossing the river before the floods came. He spoke in English but with a thick accent and I had to listen carefully to understand him.

'We go wit dem caddle, yanno, across dem ribbers before dat wader come up,' he explained. He was very animated, pointing in the directions of the rivers and Derby as he explained how the stockmen took the cattle from the stations to the city to be slaughtered. I was so enthralled by his stories that I almost forgot the job at hand. He had high blood pressure and blood sugar so, concerned he might have uncontrolled diabetes, I told him to wait to see the doctor before reluctantly moving on to my next patient.

We spent a busy day checking as many residents' health as possible before it was time to pack up. We wanted to leave by 3 pm so we could arrive in Derby before dark, but with 20 minutes to go I was asked to give a pregnant young girl the once-over. Her baby was kicking reassuringly and she promised me she was going to Fitzroy next week to see a midwife. We talked about her diet. Access to processed food high in sugar, fat and salt was thankfully limited in these communities because they were so far from towns, and I was pleased to hear she was eating plenty of bush tucker such as kangaroo, fish, native berries and yams, which is full of nutrients. I was confident all would be well.

That night, as I gave Ian a blow-by-blow account of my day, I could feel my conviction growing. I had come to Derby to get a feel for working with Aboriginal communities and now there was no doubt in my mind where I wanted to go next. I had to find a job working in the heart of the outback.

Chapter 11
A world apart

Six months in Derby raced by all too quickly. Thankfully there were no big birthing dramas in the hospital while I was there, and I loved every minute of my time. I learnt so much and it was wonderful working with so many like-minded people of various backgrounds; I developed great friendships with some of the other nurses and midwives, who'd ventured out of the city for similar reasons to mine. And I loved looking after my Aboriginal patients, who were unfailingly kind to me, remarkably tolerant of my unfamiliarity with their practices and culture, and by and large far less demanding than some women I had dealt with in Wodonga.

Ian and I decided we weren't quite done with our first outback adventure yet, so I managed to arrange a six-week posting at Kalgoorlie Hospital before we headed down to Adelaide to spend Christmas with Ian's family.

Founded in 1893 during the West Australian gold rush, Kalgoorlie has retained plenty of its character from the old days. Some 600 kilometres north-east of Perth, it still has a rough and ready feel about it, with its numerous pubs and brothels, but that makes it all the more fascinating. You can't help thinking of the history of the place and how crazy it would have been at the peak of the rush gold. With wide sweeping streets like Derby, it still has many of its original buildings, as impressive reminders of the town's early wealth.

Kalgoorlie had also been experiencing a more recent boom so while we were there we visited a 'super pit', and watched a controlled explosion of ore taking place so the gold could be extracted. Even though when we visited the global financial crisis was just hitting Kalgoorlie, and the mining industry was stepping down its production, the quality of facilities designed to attract fly-in, fly-out workers and their young families made it an especially comfortable place to call home for the short time we were there.

The hospital was about the same size as Derby's and its staff were so welcoming and friendly that it was a pleasure to go in every day. I was put to work in the postnatal and birth suites and in the special care nursery. As at Derby, we looked after a number of Aboriginal women who'd had to travel long distances from their families to give birth. This time I was better prepared and I'm sure more understanding after all I had learnt from my patients at Derby. The more I experienced in Kalgoorlie, the more I wanted to find a permanent outback post. After a busy and fulfilling six weeks, Ian and I packed up again and – somewhat reluctantly – headed east.

Fifteen months later, at 5 am on Labour Day morning, my daughter Clare was, appropriately, in labour and our lives were about to change again.

Since returning to Wodonga I'd been single-mindedly scouring the medical press for suitable outback jobs. I'd even taken a part-time practice nurse role at my sister Faye's hospital to improve my experience in women's health and sexual health counselling. Nothing would hold me back from chasing my dream now.

Then Clare announced she was pregnant. I immediately felt torn. Was this the right time to abandon my family and head off to a distant corner of the country? But my retirement was looming and I knew I would never have a better opportunity to put my skills to use while I was at the top of my game. I could all too easily miss my chance if I didn't grab it now. Even though I felt a pang of guilt for wanting to be selfish about my future, I reminded myself I had to live my life, just as my children had their futures ahead of them, to do what they wanted. I couldn't help thinking back to my own struggle between what my parents wanted and what

I wanted – to marry Ian and get on with building our life. As for Ian, he was all for the adventure, and agreed Clare would manage just fine without us, so with some trepidation I started putting in applications for remote-area jobs.

Seven months later, bleary-eyed, Ian and I opened our front door at 4.30 am after a phone call from Clare's husband, Matt. they were bothon the doorstep, Clare clutching the base of her belly. She seemed able to walk and talk through the contractions so I made her a cup of tea, got her comfortable on our chaise longue and put on a film to distract her.

During her pregnancy Clare and I had had many birthing and labour discussions – I wanted her to be as informed as possible so she could make the right decisions for her birth, but I was careful to leave those decisions to her. She was adamant she wanted a natural birth without intervention, had found a Calm Birth instructor and attended classes on relaxation. As her mum and her birth support – to both her and Matt – my plan was to keep her at the house for as long as I could, and encourage her to rest and save her strength for later.

But by later that morning Clare was frustrated that nothing much had happened and declared that she wanted to go to the hospital. So off we went. The midwife on duty told Clare she was only 3 centimetres dilated so we trooped back home to wait it out. I ran Clare a bath and for the next two hours she wallowed in the blissful weightlessness of the water.

After lunch we headed back to the hospital, only to hear she was just one more centimetre dilated than before.

Clare was exasperated with the slow progress. 'One bloody centimetre in four hours?' she huffed. 'Well, I'm not leaving.'

Poor Clare – four more uncomfortable hours passed and she'd barely made another centimetre in progress. It did seem very slow and I began to worry about the way the labour was going. Matt and Kerry Ann, their Calm Birth coach, were doing their best to get Clare in the zone, but she was far from serene.

'I've had enough of this,' she growled. 'I want my membranes ruptured.'

My heart sunk. I knew this would increase the intensity of her pain and I was scared for her. I was suddenly painfully aware of why you should never be professionally involved in a medical situation with someone you love. Unable to give impartial advice, I let her and Matt talk to Alison, their obstetric GP, and the decision was made to go ahead.

As I'd feared, Clare's contractions quickly escalated. It was awful to see her rolling on and off the bed, crying out as her body shuddered. As she stamped her feet and rocked with agitation, she had hardly a moment to relax between contractions.

'Mum, I can't do this,' she cried out at one point. 'Help me!'

Feeling sick to the stomach, I helped her to the shower and gently massaged her back as tears rolled down her cheeks.

To my dismay the relief was short-lived. 'I want an epidural,' Clare sobbed. Matt was looking at me in desperation.

I tried to keep my voice calm. 'Do you remember what you said about wanting a natural birth?' I ventured.

'I don't care what I said before,' Clare snapped. 'I want an epidural.'

Within minutes the doctor had arrived and as Clare was helped to sit up for the injection, I quietly left the room. Standing in the corridor outside the birthing room I started to sob. As much as I wanted to be strong, it was difficult. How could any mother cope with seeing her child suffer like this? I was embarrassed that I of all people could be so emotional when I'd seen women go through this procedure almost on a daily basis. I'd even supported mothers of daughters, but at that moment it felt as though none of them had reacted as I was now! But it was my little girl this time.

Whatever I was feeling, I had to pull myself together for Clare and get back in there and support her. But when I returned to the birth suite the atmosphere had totally changed: Clare was sitting up on the bed and looked happy for the first time in hours. She could still move her legs, but the pain of the contractions had dwindled. Soon Kerry Ann thought she was ready to push and we faced our next hurdle. The baby's heartbeat was dipping with each contraction so it needed to be born quickly, but Clare was exhausted.

After consulting with the doctor, Clare and Matt consented to a vacuum-assisted birth. Mentally I was already preparing for the next step – a caesarean section. I stood next to Clare as she gripped my hand, holding my breath as Alison attached the vacuum cup to the baby's head and began the suction.

'It's moving,' she told Clare. 'I'm going to give you a small cut and with the next contraction you push and I think we'll be there.'

At last the baby girl we'd all been so anxious to meet slid into Alison's hands. Relief washed over me as my first grandchild flexed her little body and let out a strong cry. Alison passed her up to Clare for a cuddle and I stood mesmerised, watching my daughter fall in love with her first child. I'd seen this tender moment of human life so many times, but this one quickly moved me to tears.

For the next few weeks little Eva thrived, feeding well and putting on weight. But Clare was getting next to no sleep and I could tell she was overcome with anxiety as a result, so we agreed I should move in temporarily. That way, when Eva woke in the night I could get up for her, change her and take her to Clare for a feed in bed.

After three nights of sleep Clare was a different woman and seemed far less overwhelmed by motherhood. After feeling so helpless at the birth, it was immensely satisfying to be able to help my beloved daughter, and the perfect introduction to my new granddaughter, just as it had been to my niece all those years ago when I'd stayed with Faye in similar circumstances.

This time, though, it was extra gratifying to hear Clare tell her friends for months afterwards that sometimes you just need your mum!

✻

A few weeks after Eva's birth, I was asked to a phone interview with the Northern Territory Department of Health to discuss a position as a remote area midwife in a community called Maningrida in Arnhem Land. Its population was a little under 3000, and of those 90 per cent were Aboriginal.

Although the interview, via a teleconference, was nerve-racking because it was with five people, all from the NT Department of Health, it seemed to go well. I was convinced that this was the job of a lifetime so I was on tenterhooks about the outcome in the days that followed.

A friend in Wodonga had lived in Maningrida, working with Aboriginal women on a community development employment program printing fabrics, and she had found the whole experience life-changing. She told me about some of the wonderful relationships she'd developed, working alongside many of the women, going with them to art exhibitions in Darwin to display their work and learning about their culture. When she heard about my interview she told me I'd love it there, and that I had the right temperament to be working in an Aboriginal community. I really didn't know what she meant by that, but it encouraged me, especially since Dianne had said the same thing.

A week later, I was offered the position. I accepted it on the spot. This was all I had hoped for and more. What a wonderful opportunity to go and live and work in this unique corner of Australia, to get back to basics and really practise my craft first-hand. And I certainly got my wish to find somewhere remote: Maningrida is 500 kilometres east of Darwin, on the north coast of the Northern Territory, completely cut off in the summer when the rains come, and non-Aboriginal people needed a special permit to visit.

Now we had to break the news to Lauren and Clare that I'd accepted a job 4120 kilometres away. By now Clare was managing well with Eva and it was reassuring that Lauren, who was working as a travel agent in Wangaratta, lived close by. But that didn't stop me from feeling guilty.

'What are we going to do without you?' Lauren asked as we spent an afternoon washing and folding laundry at Clare's. 'We only just got used to having you around again!'

'We're not dead,' I laughed. 'We'll be back!'

When Ian and I packed up the car and prepared to leave for Darwin, Lauren and Clare were there to wave us off in a teary farewell. As Ian drove us down the highway, it took at least half an hour before I stopped wiping away tears and blowing my nose.

In Darwin I was to spend a week on an orientation course. I thought of Mum and Dad and wondered what they'd have made of all this. I could imagine them saying 'Why on earth do you want go there?' And I knew what my answer would be: 'Because I want to and I can!' I was excited about what might lie ahead and really proud that Ian and I were upping sticks to share another big adventure together, instead of slowing down and resting on our laurels at this time in our lives.

So we began our expedition north. To save money we camped en route, which alone was a great adventure. Ian and I have always said, some people love five-star accommodation – we love 1,000,000-star accommodation! It's the serenity, the vibe. We just love the outdoor life, and we'd have missed the sights, sounds and sense of the changing country if we had stayed in motels.

By now we were old camping hands, and Ian made sure we had all the mod cons – his pride and joy was the shower and pump he'd installed under the bonnet of our four-wheel drive, which meant we could strip off and enjoy warm water in the middle of nowhere before the motor cooled.

One night we set up near a railway track. After our campfire dinner we settled down for the night in warm sleeping bags – no matter how scorching it is during the day, in the outback it's cold at night all year round. We slept soundly until we were woken by the ground shaking and an ominous rumble. For a terrifying second I thought we were about to be cleaned up by a road-train ploughing through our makeshift camp. But as we sat upright with pounding hearts, the lights of a huge train thundering past illuminated our tent. 'It's the Ghan!' Ian laughed, as the roaring clatter of the famous passenger train finally began to fade into the distance.

We made it to Darwin in a week. My orientation at the Royal Darwin Hospital started the very next day, and I met the directors of nursing, the sexual health team and the rheu-matic heart disease team for one-on-one chats. There was also a cultural orientation. There was a great deal to learn and it was obvious that I'd never be able to get to grips with all the intricacies and nuances of this ancient culture in such a short time, and of course the best lessons I would learn on the job. But I was determined to take in as much as I could.

The traditional landowners of the country in Central Arnhem Land are the Kunibidji people, whose language is Ndjébbana. We were told that in Maningrida 13 different languages are spoken, and most people in the community can speak at least three of these. Apparently it's possible that Maningrida is the most multilingual community in the world! The main languages spoken there are Burarra and Ndjébbana, and we were assured there would be interpreters on hand for when we needed them.

We were educated about the importance of showing respect not only for the community elders but for the ancestors who walked the lands on which we live. We were guided through the intricacies of Aboriginal family struc-tures, the complex social and marriage laws, and the kinship system, in which there are far more relationships than non-Aboriginal families have – for example, often cousins are known as brothers and sisters, and aunts and uncles may be called father and mother, and have similar roles to parents. We were also introduced to the cultural significance of various important ceremonies, such as funerals and young men's coming-of-age celebrations.

After a week of working hard to take all this in, finally we set off on the last stage of our journey. We'd hoped to drive the final leg but when we got to Darwin we discovered that wouldn't be possible – the roads were closed because of an unusually late wet season. A barge left from Darwin every week to service lots of remote communities, including Maningrida. The barge took three days to get to the town and brought in supplies for the shops; even large items such as cars and boats were transported on it when the roads were inaccessible. But unfortunately for us, it didn't allow passengers.

So we packed minimal clothing – the rest of our luggage would have to wait for Ian to fly back and retrieve the car when the roads had reopened – and the next day boarded a 20-seater plane.

Soon we were flying over the wilderness of the Northern Territory. The view from the air was breathtaking: vast, lush wetlands and muddy-looking rivers snaking their way out to the Arafura Sea. As we passed over huge grey flat rock formations – known as 'stone country' – the plane began to descend and I could see small, grid-like squares of tin rooftops poking out from the green grass of the community. I started to get butterflies – we were close to Maningrida.

After the plane taxied to a tin shed that served as the airport's office, departures, arrivals and baggage claim all rolled into one, we saw our welcoming party – a nurse from the clinic, Jenny, and Sebastian, our driver, a rotund Aboriginal man with a mop of curly black hair and a big grin.

Before we knew it we were racing towards the town. Even though I'd been prepared for its remoteness, it was a bit of a shock to see just how isolated and barren Maningrida looked. Red dust swirled around in the breeze and I noticed a pack of barking dogs chasing behind the car.

'They're not giving up easily, are they?' I said, as more and more scruffy-looking hounds joined in the race.

'Best get yourself a big stick,' Sebastian said.

'I don't think he's joking,' Ian whispered.

We gazed out of the window, taking in shabby, litter-strewn streets. At every turn we seemed to pass a rusting shell of a car lying forlornly, tyres missing, windows smashed and bonnet bent out of shape.

Sebastian pulled up outside the health clinic – a modern pale-yellow brick and corrugated iron building. The pack of hounds pursuing the car had scattered by now, but at least 15 more dogs were waiting outside the clinic doors.

'It looks like a veterinary clinic,' I said to Ian.

'*Shar! Shar!*' Jenny shouted at the dogs and one by one they stretched lazily, got to their feet and began to slope away. 'That's a word they all know,' she said.

We found out later these were camp dogs: mangy local dogs that aren't cared for properly but will follow a family member from place to place in the hope they'll get fed. They're skinny, usually full of ticks, riddled with worms, often hairless and they sometimes have visible wounds, mostly caused by fighting. Many have a dash of dingo in them. Needless to say, they were to be avoided. But that was easier said than done, as I was soon to discover.

We followed Jenny into the clinic for a quick tour. The building was divided in half, pink for women's and blue for the men's.

'It's Aboriginal culture to keep things separate,' Bernadette, an Aboriginal assistant, explained. 'When there's women's business going on, the men don't come in, and it's the same rule for men's business.'

Jenny introduced me to my new colleagues. A male doctor worked at the clinic every second week, and two female locum doctors came and went on short-term contracts. There were about 10 other nurses in the clinic, from Victoria, Western Australia, Canada and New Zealand. They all seemed pleased to have me on the team: I found out later that it was the only time there'd been five midwives in Maningrida, so the clinic was better-resourced than ever before.

The birthing room was well kitted out. Alongside an old-fashioned stainless steel delivery bed, there was other more modern apparatus, including an electronic blood pressure machine and a state-of-the-art neonatal resuscitation cot. Considering that we were 500 kilometres from the nearest hospital, all this bounty was immensely reassuring.

When I began to think about the logistics of what would need to happen in an emergency situation it dawned on me just how reliant these mothers would be on me, and that I'd been used to having back-up just minutes away. I knew that the majority of mothers-to-be were airlifted to Darwin at between 36 and 38 weeks, but would I have time to transfer a labouring woman in trouble? I wasn't familiar with all the specific ins and outs of an emergency transfer yet, and the thought was a little daunting. But this was my job and I told myself I would make sure I was ready for anything. Nevertheless, I hoped it wasn't going to be necessary to deal with major emergencies too often this far from help.

When Bernadette showed us our new accommodation, I was relieved to see that the purple duplex was nicer than the one we'd had in Derby. A decent-sized two-bedroom unit had been fitted out with quality furniture, albeit all of it covered in red dust. But for now, a little dust we could live with. Feeling shattered from the journey and all the novelties of our first day, we went straight to bed.

'I'm going to give this place a good clean tomorrow,' Ian mumbled sleepily as our heads hit the pillows.

In the middle of the night I awoke suddenly, startled by a noise. I sat upright in bed, momentarily disorientated by my surroundings. Squinting into the dark I could see that Ian was already out of bed and pulling on his trousers. 'Sshhh,' he said when he saw I was awake. 'There's someone outside.'

I clambered out of bed and tiptoed to join him by the window.

'It looks like a woman rocking a baby,' he said, peering through the flyscreen. 'I'll go and get a closer look.'

As I watched anxiously from the window, Ian went outside and shone a torch across the back verandah. 'What are you doing?' he asked as the torch cast a spotlight on a startled-looking couple. From their half-dressed state the answer was immediately apparent.

'I don't think you should be here,' Ian told them firmly. 'You better go somewhere else.'

We found out later that our house had been empty for a while. With many households in Maningrida occupied by around 10 to 20 people, I guess this young couple had been trying to snatch some privacy.

The next morning Ian and I were laughing about our twilight visitors, when I suddenly caught a glimpse of another early-morning intruder in our backyard – a full-sized Brahman bull munching on a white linen shirt I'd just hung out!

We managed to shoo the bull away and retrieve my poor shirt, now pitted with teeth marks and covered in grassy slime. I later discovered that the bull was called Ozzie and lived in a house across the road as a 'pet'. After that I'd often see him strolling around with a tea towel or a t-shirt hanging out of his mouth, and we were careful never to leave our gate open again.

Ozzie's partner in crime was a scar-skinned camp dog. Ozzie would happily knock over bins so the dastardly duo could forage for scraps of food. Any time we heard a loud commotion from outside we were pretty sure who the culprits were.

As it was my first day, I decided to take a drive to see a bit more of the town before I started work at the clinic. The weather in Maningrida that day was not dissimilar to

Derby's: a balmy breeze gave the illusion the heat might
be bearable, but if you strayed into the direct sun it was
way, way too hot. It was autumn so the rains had stopped,
but most days it got up to at least 30 degrees and was
extremely humid.

The town was spread out along sealed roads that were in
various states of disrepair. Most of the homes were made of
either corrugated iron or brick and had louvred windows.
It was early, but there were plenty of people out, many
wandering around barefoot. Not surprisingly I saw very few
white faces. The women were dressed in brightly coloured
skirts with t-shirts and the men tended to wear over-sized
board shorts or jeans. As an outsider I felt there was a sort of
brooding atmosphere to the town, which I put down to the
heat, the obvious poverty, and the fact that it was all so new
to me.

At the clinic, a woman had arrived in labour. When I
heard this, my stomach lurched. So much for births being
infrequent! Of course, as an experienced midwife, usually
that would be no cause for alarm, but I was definitely
feeling a bit unsettled by my new surroundings, and still
coming to grips with being so far from help in an emergency. I'd been told that many of the Aboriginal women I'd
see would be anaemic and couldn't afford to lose too much
blood at birth, so if a woman were to end up giving birth
in the clinic rather than in Darwin, preventing a post-partum haemorrhage needed to be in the forefront of my mind
right from the start. Still, one step at a time – I forced

myself to push all the worst-case scenarios to the back of my mind and followed Trisha, the clinic nurse on duty, to the birthing room.

Inside, I found a young Aboriginal girl called Daphne, who was 37 weeks pregnant with her second baby. I asked why she hadn't made it to Darwin, and Janet, a remote area nurse who'd been dealing with all the antenatal care up until now, told me she'd been living at an outstation. 'Outstation' refers to the place in which a traditional land owner has a house or houses for his family. Around Maningrida there were outstations distanced anything between 20 and 150 kilometres outside the town.

'I spotted her yesterday and asked her to come to clinic,' Janet told me. Daphne had gone into labour before her transfer could be arranged and she was now too far along to be evacuated for the birth.

Introducing myself, I put an IV line in her arm and asked to examine her. She was well on her way, about 6 centimetres dilated. Her baby bump felt small for 37 weeks – it should have measured 37 centimetres from the pubic bone to the top of the uterus, but Daphne was measuring 33 centimetres. This could have meant her dates were wrong and she was in fact carrying a 33-week-old baby, or that her baby was small for its dates because it hadn't had its nutritional fill in the uterus. All babies who weighed less than 2500 grams had to be transferred to Darwin to be supervised, to ensure they had the best nutritional start and began gaining weight as soon as possible.

As Janet called Darwin to liaise with a medical team, Daphne let out a squeal of pain.

'I need to push!' she cried.

Checking between her legs I could already see the dark hair on her baby's head. Everything was happening so quickly. Janet stood primed with the resuscitation kit as the head emerged, and I smiled with relief to hear Daphne's new baby girl let out a hearty cry. She weighed just 2 kilograms.

I rubbed Daphne's tummy to make sure her uterus remained contracted. All seemed well, and when the retrieval team – a midwife and a flight doctor – arrived an hour later we were ready for them. We accompanied Daphne to the dusty airfield and watched as mother and baby were helped onboard and the doors of the Air Med plane slammed shut. The engines fired up and the small aircraft sped along the runway, lifting into the sky as we waved them off.

'I think you're going to like it here, Beth,' Trisha said. I had been thinking exactly the same thing.

Chapter 12
Maningrida time

Armed with a sawn-off broom handle as a dog stick – Ian's solution to the motley band of mangy creatures that inevitably emerged slavering whenever we left the house – I set off on my walk to work. Sure enough, within a few minutes I heard ominous snarling as a pack of mongrels came hurtling around the side of a house and started tearing the living daylights out of each other in front of me. I back-pedalled in fright, brandishing my stick in what I hoped was a menacing manner, and praying that they couldn't sense my fear.

To my enormous relief, a thin man appeared, waving his arms in the air. 'Shar, Shar, Shar!' he bellowed. The dogs immediately stopped their ruckus and slunk off. Still shaking, I thanked him and set off again, a little less confidently. I hoped I could learn fast to be as effective as he was at beating back these hounds or walking to work every day was going to be an exercise in terror.

Once I had recovered sufficiently to take in what was around me, I could see that most of the houses in my new neighbourhood had been built from kits, which must have been transported to the community by barge or road, and it seemed that their inhabitants spent a lot of time outside around fires. The streets were scattered with litter and every so often I'd catch the pungent waft of stale rubbish from an upturned bin, felled, no doubt, by a scavenging dog.

Still reeling from coming face to face with the terrifying local dog entourage, when I arrived at the clinic I asked Janet how the camp dogs had become such a problem. 'Those big packs loosely belong to different families and come and go as they please. If there's any kind of commotion, they instinctively assume food is involved and attack each other to get to it. Humans, too. It's awful. Wait till you see the bites we have to treat.'

I shuddered at how close I had come to finding out this morning. And now that I had raised it, it was clear that this was just one of the many daily trials that was wearing Janet down. She admitted she was at her wits' end with life in Maningrida. 'I'm happy this is my last day,' she confessed. 'I've had enough.' I later discovered that it was no wonder, as Janet had been shouldering much more day to day than anyone realised, and her stress levels must have been off the chart. It turned out that she'd been on call constantly since she'd arrived in the community – both as a regular and ante-natal nurse. 'It was too much,' she said. She must have seen my expression, as she quickly added that it would be better for me just doing the midwifery care.

'She seemed very stressed,' I told Ian worriedly as we sat on the verandah that evening. 'I hope that isn't me after a year!'

It was surreal to look out on the strange world I could see from my new home. Everything was so foreign and utterly different from Wodonga. The air was rich with the smell of burning native pine and we could see families huddled around fires to cook, eat and keep warm. With the sound of didger-idoo, clap sticks and Aboriginal people calling out in their native language, it was like being in another country.

The next morning I arrived at the clinic early, bright-eyed and bushy-tailed, eager to prepare for my first day running the antenatal clinic. After all the build-up at taking on a new challenge, I was disappointed to find just three women sitting in the waiting room.

Hoping that more would arrive – it was only 10 am, after all – I ushered in my first expectant mother. Jo was 12 weeks pregnant with her first baby. When I asked her to lie on the examination couch she looked reluctant. 'I don't want you,' she eventually said. 'I want Janet.'

'Janet's gone,' I said.

'But I don't like you,' she replied.

'That's okay,' I said. 'You don't have to like me. Let's see how your baby is getting on.'

I spent a good twenty minutes with her, doing a thorough check – taking her blood pressure, checking her urine and enquiring about her health. She answered my questions grudgingly and looked pleased when I walked her out to find an empty waiting room.

'What happened to the other two ladies?' I asked.

'Dunno,' she shrugged, with what looked very much like a smirk.

I was at a loss, and more than a little dismayed that my first day was beginning to look like a complete washout. Maybe they'll come back, I thought, trying to be optimistic. But thirty minutes later my waiting room was still empty and deathly quiet.

'Everything okay?' Hellen, the clinic manager, asked when she checked on me. I told her what had happened – just one woman to see when I was expecting eight. She didn't look as concerned as I felt. She simply asked me who I was looking for. After I'd run through the names on my list, she showed me a map of the town pinned to the wall and pointed to roughly where each woman's home was. 'You should drive round and look for them,' she said.

Wow! In my entire career I'd never had to round up my patients before. Wasn't it a little intrusive to go looking for mums-to-be? How would they take an unfamiliar white clinic worker turning up at their home? Oh, come on, Beth. You came to Maningrida to get out of your comfort zone,

I reminded myself. I had to make a start with the community somehow, and if this was the best way to do so, then there was no time like the present. I wasn't going to be much help to anyone if I didn't have any patients.

So, with the crucial map on my lap, I drove around the town until I found the home of one of my missing mothers. Half a dozen dogs rushed onto the porch barking territorially. We'd been warned by the clinic manager not to get out of the car in certain parts of the town where 'cheeky' dogs roamed. Far from being cute and perky, as the name suggests, cheeky dogs are the ones known to be aggressive and territorial. So I tooted the horn and waited for someone to come to the door. After a couple of minutes, a sleepy-looking man emerged.

'Lucy here?' I asked.

'No. Lucy at blue house, top camp. Upstairs house,' he told me.

Right. I had no idea how to follow his instructions, and after driving round and stopping at two blue houses nearby, I was no nearer to finding Lucy. I headed back to the clinic. There I spoke to a helpful health worker who knew exactly where Lucy lived. 'In the blue house with two steps out front,' he smiled.

Thanks to his handy description, I finally found the house, sounded my horn and waited for someone to come to the door. The woman who emerged told me she was Lucy's mother. Great! Finally my wild goose chase was getting somewhere.

'Lucy at warehouse,' she said. After a bit of thought, I decided she must mean the supermarket and it didn't seem practical to make my way there and ask around for her. I pressed my head to the steering wheel in frustration. Was it going to be like this with all the women in my care, I wondered. I drove back to the clinic exhausted and rather disheartened.

'You're finding your feet in a new place,' Ian said later. 'Once the women get to know you, they'll come.'

After all that, at least one of us had had a good day. That afternoon Ian had got a job driving a forklift for the general store.

The following morning I was in the midst of organising my paperwork when a shy young woman peered around the door of the consulting room. It was Lucy! 'You looking for me?' she asked. I could have kissed her.

'Welcome to Maningrida time,' Hellen joked later. 'Everything is very laidback here. Messages often get passed through half a dozen family members before they get to the right person. But you do get there eventually.'

She was right. After a few weeks of doing the hard yards of tracking down, rounding up and talking to the pregnant women in the town, I had a grand total of 22 antenatal patients. Success at last!

My newly acquired flock of patients were mostly aged between 17 and 22. Many had other children and had first become pregnant when they were just 15 or 16. Given that the majority of these mothers were so young, it was disturbing to find many suffering ill health. Of the 22 young women on my books in those first months, four were diabetic, two were on monthly injections of penicillin for rheumatic heart disease and one was epileptic (the first I knew of this was when she arrived at the clinic door and had a fit). Almost all weighed no more than 60 kilograms. In Wodonga there'd been so much emphasis on the problems of obese women having babies, with special seminars and the like, that it seemed strange to be looking after so many women who were actually underweight. It was soon obvious that many women here grew up suffering from a lack of nutrition.

Statistically, the facts are sadly clear. Aboriginal women suffer worse health than the rest of the population, and that has a lot to do with poverty. Living in impoverished and overcrowded conditions is detrimental to good health. The women with rheumatic heart disease had likely become ill after childhood scabies had gone untreated. Unfortunately scabies in Maningrida was rife: statistically seven out of 10 children in the town would likely contract it before their first birthday. I was already seeing babies as young as six weeks old suffering the condition.

Scabies is caused by tiny mites burrowing under the skin and triggering a severe rash that's relentlessly itchy. The mite, which spreads from skin-to-skin contact, can be caught in any environment, but the bugs thrive in crowded living spaces where bedding or clothing is shared. Unfortunately, many of the homes I visited were cramped and dirty, with discarded bottles, chip packets, lolly wrappers and even dog faeces on the floor. (It was no wonder that many of the women also had worms.) Sometimes up to 12 adults were living in a relatively small house, and the floors of living areas were often completely occupied by mattresses. This made it near impossible to carry out a proper clean unless the occupants of the home pulled the mattresses outside, where the sunlight would kill the mites. Whenever I had the opportunity, I would urge mothers to do this, and also to wash all the bedding and their children with soap and water.

It was distressing to find a newborn baby with a red, itchy rash on their hands and feet, fast spreading up their back, but the sad truth is that because scabies is so contagious it is very hard to get rid of in such a close-knit community. Nonetheless, some headway has been made in Maningrida, thanks to a team from a non-profit organisation called One Disease. Their clinicians spent six months in the community carrying out screenings and treatment, and educating the population house by house. Their ultimate aim is to raise a million dollars through fundraising to eradicate scabies in the town in the next seven years.

As so many of my patients were underweight and some were anaemic, one of my major priorities was to try to help them make better food choices and adopt a healthier lifestyle. But, as I had learnt from trying to re-educate obese patients in the past, it's a major challenge to make anyone change the habits of a lifetime. Even more so when, time and again, I'd make an appointment with someone to discuss these issues, only to find they didn't turn up.

Eventually I realised I had to try a different tactic. Between 24 and 28 weeks, mothers-to-be had to have a gestational diabetes screening. This involved testing their blood-sugar levels, and the women were expected to stay in the clinic for the two hours it took to complete the test. So this window of time was my opportunity. While my temporary charges were able to use that period to relax at the clinic, I could have a one-on-one chat with them, so hopefully they'd leave with a better understanding of what happens to the body during birth and what they should be eating to keep their strength up and have a healthy baby.

As I got to know the women in my care, I discovered that many of them had a limited understanding of how to nurture their bodies in this way during pregnancy. And eventually I realised that advice I would usually give to expectant mothers about diet and nutrition also had limited application in some cases. For example, even for those who might be interested in trying to prepare the nutritious meals I suggested, the reality was that the majority of homes didn't have kitchens as I'd know them. Generally if they even had a stove it was broken; most had no form of refrigeration. The shops did sell fresh produce, but it only came in once a week, having been on a barge for three days already. Lack of money was also forever a problem; and it was ingrained in these women to share their food, even if they had to go without themselves. So the easier and cheaper options in the shops were finger food, fast food and soft drinks – chips, fried chicken and fish washed down with litre-bottles of Coke. Not the ideal diet for anyone, never mind an expectant mum.

As I'd discovered in Derby, it was no coincidence that the mums-to-be whose families still hunted and gathered in the traditional way, and therefore had access to freshly caught fish and seafood, or iron-rich kangaroo and buffalo meat, were in much better prenatal health. Likewise, the women who went out hunting crabs not only got a healthy dose of omega-3 and vitamin B but benefited from the exercise. So my stock question to women at their antenatal checks would be to ask if there was someone in their family who could take them out fishing and hunting. 'The fresher the food, the better it is for you,' I found myself saying over and over.

One Friday morning I arrived at the clinic to find a heavily pregnant woman standing at the door of my consulting room. I didn't recognise her, but Hellen had warned me that women sometimes slipped through the net.

'We have women who live out bush at a family out-station,' she explained. 'If they don't come into town, we don't know about them. Other times, women hide away because they don't want to be flown out to Darwin at thirty-six weeks. They don't like being separated from their families.'

Not wanting to be apart from your family at a time like that is something any expectant mother could understand. The Northern Territory state health authority only paid for an escort if a woman was under 18, so in time I learnt to be creative in finding a reason for a first-time mother to have an approved escort. The majority of Maningrida families could not afford the extra airfare to Darwin, so transport out of the community was understandably not a practical or appealing prospect.

My new patient's name was Tina and she looked full term to me. Her medical history showed she'd had four babies. I asked if she'd had normal births.

'They cut me to take that baby out,' she smiled.

'For all of them?' I asked. She nodded.

Oh Lord. I measured Tina's stomach. Her fundal height was 42 centimetres: she was due any moment and she was going to need a caesarean. Any mother-to-be who's had more than one previous caesarean cannot give birth vaginally without enormous risk. The biggest potential problem was that a vaginal birth would result in Tina's uterus rupturing, as the scar tissue might well give way during labour, resulting in the loss of the baby and sometimes the mother. The other serious risk was that the placenta could embed deeply into her uterine scar, making its eventual removal very compli-cated, which could result in a massive haemorrhage.

I had to get Tina out of the community this instant so that an obstetric surgeon could perform her caesarean in a proper operating theatre. I called Darwin and arranged for her to be on a plane within a few hours. Tina started contracting on the way into Darwin and was rushed in for a caesarean section that very evening. That was one birth I was glad not to have on my watch!

The next week we had five patients booked for ultra-sounds with a sonographer who was flying into Maningrida for the day. Some scans took a while, and now I knew my pregnant charges better, I also knew that keeping them in the clinic long enough to undergo these important checks on the development of their babies would be no mean feat.

I decided I'd guard the waiting room myself to dissuade any restless mothers from leaving. Sure enough, within half an hour of opening, I spotted Jo, the teenager who'd preferred my predecessor, Janet, trying to slope away. She told me she was hungry. 'I'll come back tomorrow,' she said.

I promised to fetch her a sandwich and guided her back to her seat. She was soon called in and 40 minutes later an altogether more excited Jo came bounding out, clutching an ultrasound photo.

'My bub is as big as a mango!' she said, proudly holding out the picture for me to examine. I was delighted she seemed to be thawing towards me, and together we walked to the door.

'Pet, can I ask a question?' she suddenly asked me, a little cautiously. Of course, I told her. 'Can I have sex when I'm pregnant?' she whispered.

'You certainly can,' I smiled. 'Quite often you feel hornier when you're pregnant.'

She began to giggle. 'I just was wondering,' she said. 'I've never asked anyone before.'

For the rest of the morning I watched over the waiting room like a hawk, handing out fruit and sandwiches and putting on *Shrek* to keep the women entertained – something light and funny seemed the order of the day. By early after-noon all the ultrasounds had been completed and I left for the day with a feeling of satisfaction. I was especially pleased with myself to have been able to help Jo in a small but signif-icant way, and hopefully gain her trust a little more.

I was still learning my way around my job when I met Nina, a petite Aboriginal woman who was 12 weeks pregnant with her fourth baby.

'I want another boy this time,' she said with a big smile. 'I have two girls and a boy.'

'I might have a spare one out the back in the cabbage patch,' I joked as she covered her mouth and giggled.

When it came to her antenatal checks, Nina was a breath of fresh air, always keen to attend and even calling through the window to me if the clinic hadn't yet opened. Her voice was very distinct – deeper than the other women's. It was only after she had called out ''Ellooo, Pet!' many times to me that I realised this wasn't just a standard greeting – it was my name! Many people had trouble pronouncing Beth, so they simply called me 'Pet' instead. And it had caught on so there was no going back.

As it happened Nina lived almost opposite Ian and me. After her first visit, I often spotted her and her lovely children outside their home. Some days as I walked home from the clinic I'd see her two eldest, Krystal and Kurt, playing a game with a wheel of a broken baby stroller. They each had a stick, which they used to send the rolling wheel spinning back and forth to one another. Their ingenuity and ability to entertain themselves seemed a refreshing change from kids I saw back home, who depended more on their parents, or an endless supply of electronic games and toys, to keep them occupied.

Ian and I celebrated our third month in the town with a precious glass of wine on our verandah. To combat alcohol-related incidents and abuse in the community, no adult can buy alcohol without a permit, and ours had taken ten weeks to arrive, so this long-awaited glass of wine was savoured with reverence.

Alcohol was brought into Maningrida via a fortnightly barge delivery and each adult was entitled to purchase a maximum of six bottles of wine and 24 of mid- or light-strength beer. To cover a two-week stint of 'responsible drinking', that struck me as a lot of alcohol, and indeed it was not unusual for things to get a lot more animated on the night of the barge delivery. You had to collect your alcohol by 9.30 am. By 11 am some people had polished off more than their fair share. Some would take their stash out of the community; others would drink it as quickly as possible so they didn't have to share it with family who didn't have a permit.

If you were involved in any kind of alcohol-related incident you could lose your permit; nonetheless, fights could be heard when drunken arguments broke out, and often the police would appear. The nurses on call at the clinic on those days usually had to come out to patch up people with injuries sustained from fights. Generally by 11 pm the calls would have tailed off as the majority of the grog had been drunk.

✳

As the build-up to the wet season began, temperatures soared and the town became unbearably hot and sticky. Shrieks of laughter filled our street as Nina's kids splashed and frolicked in an inflatable pool outside their home. It was too hot to walk to work and, driving around, revelling in the car's air-conditioning, I saw children cooling off in eskies, wheelbarrows and even a wheelie bin.

While my car, consulting room and home thankfully all had air-conditioning, during house calls I really began to suffer from the heat. Within five minutes I'd feel like the Wicked Witch of the West ('I'm melting! I'm melting!') as my shirt stuck to my back and perspiration trickled down my neck.

As November approached, the humidity became more and more intense and stifling. There had been no rain up here since we'd arrived in May, but now big, black cumulus clouds began to cast shadows. For days on end they continued to roll in. Then one afternoon the sky grew eerily dark just after 2. It seemed like the end of the world was coming. As I finished up at work, I heard an ominous rumble of thunder.

After I'd scurried home to beat the downpour, Ian and I took a seat on the verandah to watch the storm as it settled in. We waved at Nina and her family, who were huddled under a tree opposite. A light pitter-patter of rain began, and Krystal and Kurt ran out squealing as the raindrops splashed on their skin. Nina's husband, Chris, followed them with the couple's 18-month-old daughter, Carla, on his shoulders. The toddler giggled with delight, flapping her hands in the air, until an almighty clap of thunder spooked us all – Kurt jumped like a startled gazelle and ran to cling to his father's legs.

What had started out as a gentle shower soon became a roof-pounding deluge that lasted for days. Suddenly I understood why the clinic had no spouting or guttering. The rain was just too heavy. The roads out of the community were closed immediately and Maningrida was put on high alert for extreme weather.

The wet season in the north of Australia often comes hand in hand with high winds, and there are usually one or two cyclones a year. Some blow out to sea or cause monsoonal rain; others cause massive destruction. In the past few weeks, locals had regaled us with horror stories of Cyclone Monica, which had pounded Maningrida for 12 hours in 2006. Winds had torn through the community at 170 kilometres an hour, snapping and uprooting trees, sending rubbish bins spinning and turning sheets of iron and timber into deadly missiles that speared buildings. Amazingly, no one had been hurt. Each year since, the town has orchestrated a massive clean-up of its streets before the wet season, as a pre-emptive measure. Workers from the local shire join emergency service response groups to remove car frames, general rubbish and any other debris that could be swept up in a storm.

After weeks of relentless downpours, the atmosphere could become pretty oppressive. Occasionally there'd be a break when I could venture out in a clinic vehicle to find a couple of women for their checks, or to deliver a message that someone needed to travel into Darwin. Ian and I were lucky that we could keep our air-conditioning running in the wet season – as a remote area nurse one of the perks was not having to pay our electricity bill. Still, everything we owned become damp, and stayed damp and musty for months at a time. Our towels wouldn't dry, and you had to fight the onset of mould every day. After a few weeks of our first wet season, we found our car's interior covered in it. From then on we put a moisture absorber in the car, which thankfully seemed to solve the problem.

One evening in mid-December I'd just finished dinner when I heard Nina's distinctive voice outside the house. 'Pet, help me!'

Rushing outside I found her being supported by Chris.

'Pet, the baby's coming,' Nina said. 'It's too early!'

Nina was 34 weeks pregnant. We rushed to my car and as we drove to the clinic I did my best to reassure her that lots of babies of that age did well. As soon as we'd arrived I helped Nina to the birthing room, phoned for a colleague and lodged an emergency call with Darwin for assistance.

Nina's fourth child was the speediest yet, emerging in an effortless way that made birth look almost easy. To our great relief the baby, while small, was breathing well. Not only that, but Nina got the precious boy she wanted. She called him Charles. As she guided him to her breast he showed no signs of distress, but both mother and baby would fly to Darwin that night so little Charles could be cared for in Darwin Hospital's special care nursery until he got bigger.

While Charles was being prepared to be transferred, I escorted Nina to the bathroom and headed back to the birth suite. Ten minutes later I went to check on her, but the toilet was empty. I scoured the clinic. She wasn't there.

'She asked to go outside,' a colleague told me. 'I think she's gone for a smoke.'

But outside there was no sign of Nina. With panic rising, I did a quick tour of the area in my car, finally pulling up outside her house. I ran to the door and was greeted by her. She was clutching a small suitcase and looked surprised to see me.

'Where have you been?' I asked.

'I had to get my bag,' she said.

I almost laughed. Nina had walked a kilometre just an hour or so after giving birth! Suffice to say I insisted on driving her back. By 2 am she and Charles were safely aboard the flight to Darwin and I had dragged my weary body to bed.

Nina and Charles returned to the community four weeks later, hale and hearty, just in time for Christmas, and an alarming cyclone warning. As everyone battened down the hatches, we braced ourselves for a storm that was presently wreaking havoc 300 kilometres away.

For the entire weekend the rain hammered down, producing about 300 millimetres of water, which quickly turned the roads into flooded waterways. I was amazed to see a red river streaming past our house – rainwater mixed with the rusty-coloured soil of the town. Remarkably, no one's home was flooded, but the foundation slabs of some houses under construction were severely undermined by the deluge of water.

Once we knew we'd escaped a direct hit, Nina's older children were soon outside, splashing about with glee as they used scrappy pieces of wood or plastic as makeshift boogie boards to float down the street.

The cyclone had cleared the skies just in time for a calm Christmas and, pleased to have escaped our first bout of extreme weather unscathed, we joined the Maningrida 'orphans' (the white folk from the clinic who were away from their family) for a gargantuan feast of ham on the bone, baked snapper, prawns, mud crab and roasted vegetables, rounded off with Christmas pudding and cake.

Nothing like a near disaster to give you an appetite!

Chapter 13
Bush business

New Year opened with a splash of colour and plenty of movement, and an unexpected new insight into Aboriginal culture. On New Year's morning we awoke to the sound of pumping dance music. Venturing out to investigate, we came across what looked like white clusters of powder speckled across the red soil and followed the trail. Then we saw a group of local Aboriginals dancing joyously in bare feet outside one of the houses. Several of the men were dressed in women's skirts and crop tops, their hair, faces and bodies dusted in flour. Their audience obviously enjoyed their performance almost as much as they did. As they gyrated enthusiastically to the music, a huddle of delighted children stood giggling.

Then one of the men shimmied over to Ian and me, grinning mischievously. There were shrieks of laughter from the kids as he pelted us smack in the face with a flour bomb.

We spluttered and laughed in surprise, batting away the cloud of flour and shaking the white dust from our clothes and hair. We later discovered that these men are called 'sistergirls'. Sistergirls are born male but identify as female. As such, they usually have the same roles as the women in the community – they hunt with the women and spend time with the women, and look after younger family members such as nieces and nephews as though they're their own. They've always been part of Aboriginal communities, although they're not always accepted by their families. In fact often the older people, who are more connected to traditional Aboriginal culture and ways of thinking, are more accepting of them than others who may have developed more unfortunate contemporary prejudices.

Aboriginal life revolves around ceremony and tradition, and hardly a day in the community seemed to pass without some kind of ritual being initiated. I'd sometimes heard the distant, mournful cries and clap sticks of 'funeral business'. However, it wasn't until mourners congregated outside the clinic that I saw close up how harrowing and punishing these Aboriginal ceremonies for the recently deceased can be, not only emotionally but physically. When I arrived at work one morning, a crowd of obviously distressed Aboriginal people was outside. The women were crying and wailing, their children alongside them, as the men stood in the background, clearly grief-stricken.

I asked an Aboriginal health worker what on earth was happening, and what we could do to help. 'A young fellow passed away overnight,' he said. 'The family's here in grief. They're waiting for the body.'

The boy was just 21 and had died at the clinic the night before, from a suspected heart attack. Suddenly the doors opened and family members appeared, carrying the boy's body in a shroud with the help of some of the clinic staff. As the sad little entourage carried their precious cargo slowly to the ambulance, a woman ran forward and slammed her body violently to the ground. I covered my mouth with my hand in shock as two other women from the family did the same. They didn't seem to care if they injured themselves.

'This is sorry business,' my colleague explained. 'The women hurt themselves because they are sorry for the death. Sometimes they make cuts on their skin too, which aren't to be stitched unless there's major bleeding or tendon damage.'

As the three heartbroken women lay crying inconsolably on the ground, I felt tears escaping from my own eyes. Seeing them hurt themselves to show the depth of their grief was deeply distressing to watch.

The ambulance began a slow trundle towards the airport – from there a plane would take the body to Darwin for an autopsy (there is no morgue in Maningrida). Stumbling to their feet, the women joined other family members to walk behind the vehicle, their heads bent low in sorrow.

'We can't open for business yet,' my colleague warned. 'The family needs to smoke the building of evil spirits.'

Three hours later, the family members returned to smoke the clinic. We watched silently as male relatives of the boy lit a fire. A sombre refrain started up on didgeridoos and clap sticks, and one of the men placed a leaf-covered branch in the fire. When smoke began to waft from the foliage, he retrieved the branch from the flames and carried it into the building, tapping the walls and doors with the smoking leaves. Only when he was satisfied that each room had been cleansed sufficiently, did the music stop and the clinic open.

Since Nina had returned to the community, I'd enjoyed watching Charles grow from a tiny sleepy newborn to a contented chubby baby, and getting to know Nina better. She often brought Charles over for a cuddle on the porch and we'd sit chatting about all sorts of things, including the many things I still had to learn about Aboriginal life. I had so many questions and Nina was very kind and patient with me. Nina's family had taken advantage of some of the educational opportunities available for community children: her parents had followed her teacher's suggestion and applied for a scholarship for her to a boarding school in Darwin, where Nina had learnt to read and write.

'Lots of people don't take these opportunities,' she told me sadly. 'They're suspicious of white culture.'

I often wondered what the Aboriginals in Maningrida really thought about all the 'balandas' (white people) who descended on their community with fresh-faced enthusiasm and idealistic plans to help, and more often than not had little or no idea about how the community worked or how to implement their grand plans. Some learnt quickly, others fell by the wayside.

'We call you "white goods",' Nina laughed. 'When one breaks down and gets worn out, we just get another one!'

I only had to embark on another round of home visits to be reminded of how and why blindly pushing white ideologies onto Indigenous communities had such limited success. With thousands of years of culture connecting Aboriginal people to the land, was it really that surprising that the homes and lifestyles we considered so much a part of the Australian dream were not their dream? As Nina explained, the material wealth and fancy homes white Australians strive for are just not a priority for people who feel such a connection with the land.

To help me understand how deep that connection to traditional life still runs, Nina invited me to attend her 12-year-old son Kurt's 'young man' ceremony. 'It symbolises Kurt's entry to manhood,' she explained. I was bowled over. I couldn't have asked for a more welcome vote of confidence than to be allowed to attend such an important celebration. Though Nina wouldn't have talked to me about men's business, I believe a boy approaching puberty is introduced into manhood with a series of initiations, which are tests of his worth and courage and designed to teach him obedience, self-discipline and the ability to be a hardworking member of the community. They can include ceremonial markings on the skin, nose piercing, circumcision, even sleep deprivation. After these are completed, ceremonies are held to celebrate his new status.

For the first step of Kurt's young man ceremony, the family brought in piles of sand to be strewn across the dirt beside Nina's house. Finding a shady spot under a tree, I could see a bare-chested Kurt sitting cross-legged on the ground, very still. His chest and face were painted with delicate lines of white and red ochre. A feather lanyard adorned his neck and he was crowned with a wreath of gum leaves. Sitting next to him were some older teenagers and two men – one who began playing clap sticks, the other the didgeridoo. They wore brightly coloured material wrapped around their hips and between their legs, and their chest, back, legs and arms were painted in white ochre.

As the level and beat of the music intensified, the group of men began to dance, moving closer and closer to Kurt. They stomped their feet in the sand to the beat of the clap sticks and occasionally stopped suddenly in a warrior pose, piercing the air with an imaginary spear. The dance ended with a final stomp just in front of Kurt and a chorus of 'Oi!' as the music also stopped.

When the music began again, the men regrouped and repeated their dance, only this time they imitated an emu, hands raised to make beaks as they jerked forwards in small pecking movements. Next came the kangaroo, the dancers holding their hands together as they jumped forwards, sticking out their necks. All this time the women of the family continued dancing in the background. I spotted Nina engrossed in the music as she swayed with her hands out in front of her and softly kicked the sand to the beat. The whole scene was breathtaking – I felt so privileged to have been invited and felt that I must have come a long way to receive such a generous show of trust.

With Nina's help, and time and patience, I felt I was slowly beginning to earn the trust of the Aboriginal women in the community. But they could still be reluctant to come to the clinic, so I'd often ask Nina if she could tell me where someone lived.

'Why don't I come with you?' she suggested one day. 'Chris can watch the children.'

Ten minutes later we were driving around and stopping outside certain houses as she called out in her own language to the women I needed to see. Nina certainly worked her magic – that day was busier than ever.

Thankfully she stepped in to help me many times after that, and I'd always have more women if she was with me to gather them up. She was also brilliant when I was having an antenatal group session because she knew people's family ties and where everyone lived, and where to track them down pronto. If a woman wasn't at her own house and I'd been told she was at 'Marta's house', without Nina it was well-nigh impossible for me to find Marta's house. There are no street names in the town, just lot numbers painted on each house, but most people don't remember offhand who lives at which number. You need to know by sight, and you obviously need to know which street the lot is on. In the absence of formal names, the streets are referred to in various ways that no one but a local could have a hope of identifying, and even then it could be a struggle. There is Airport Road, which is easy enough. Then there's Middle Road Top Camp, Cyclone Ally, Top Shop and Bottom Shop. The map of the town almost has its own language.

So Nina's local knowledge was priceless – she would instantly know where a particular woman might be and would help me navigate the roads to find her. She'd even stay afterwards and prepare afternoon tea with me for the participants of the class. It became clear that she held a position of great respect among the women of the community and I became ever more grateful that she'd taken it upon herself to befriend me.

The longer I worked with the women of Maningrida, the more I came to understand the difference between their attitude to pregnancy and the one I had grown up with. For them, pregnancy is not something they flaunt or tell the world about. It is women's business, and women's business is private. For example, it is rare to see an obviously pregnant woman socialising or even buying groceries at the shop. I also noticed that the women seemed reluctant to sit in the general waiting room at the clinic where other patients could see them. Instead, they'd congregate in the smaller waiting area in the women's end of the clinic.

Now that I knew why it took a lot of effort for a mother-to-be to seek me out, I had made a habit of leaving my office door open if I was between patients or doing paperwork. That way, anyone who was hesitant or reluctant to come and see me could slip in without having to register at reception or put their name on a waiting list.

One day I was working at my computer when a tall young woman with a little girl on her hip peered around my door. Introducing herself as Leona, she announced she was here for a check-up. She promptly took a seat beside my desk, lifting her daughter on to her knee. The toddler was thin like her mother, with big, dark brown eyes and long eyelashes.

'This is Ceira,' Leona said, smiling as the little girl put her hand down her mother's top and helped herself to a breast.

Having established that Leona was 13 weeks pregnant with her second baby, and after completing the business of my usual checks, I offered to drop her home as I was heading back to the house for lunch.

'Is this your car?' Leona asked as we made our way to her house. 'It's nice,' she said. 'Can you take me fishing?'

Leona wanted to go fishing on an outstation about 30 kilometres out of town, on the Cadell River. It wasn't like I had other plans for the weekend, nor was I about to pass up the perfect opportunity to watch and learn how she fished and what she'd catch, so I happily agreed.

On Saturday morning I got up early, baked a batch of scones and packed them in a picnic basket with chocolate cake, tea and coffee. I arrived at Leona's home at 10 and tooted the horn. She eventually stumbled out with Ceira, both looking sleepy. In they got and Leona directed me to her mother's house. There we found her mother, father, boyfriend and four more children who wanted to join us.

I explained that I only had room for three people in the back – I didn't have enough seatbelts for any more. It was decided that the children would have to miss out and I was dismayed when the little ones began to cry. I felt terrible but I couldn't cave in and take them; if I had an accident I'd never forgive myself, and of course I'd be responsible.

Our next stop was out of town at the house of a traditional landowner. 'We need to get his permission to go to his country,' Leona explained.

He seemed to have no qualms about granting it, and five minutes later we pulled up beside a patch of boggy land by the river, thick with mangroves. While the men headed off to fish, holding Ceira's hand I followed Leona and her mother towards some thick shrubs to hunt for mud mussels, which you find in the mud flats of the Kimberley and all the way down the east coast to Brisbane.

We were met by a literal wall of mosquitoes. I'd applied half a ton of Aerogard that morning, but the mozzies were apparently unfazed by it, and battling through their assault was horrible. I couldn't see to walk, let alone watch anyone fish. In the end it was too much and I had to admit defeat, somewhat shamefacedly, to Leona, who seemed unperturbed. We agreed I'd take Ceira back to the car and wait there with her.

Back in the safety of the Nissan, I sang songs to keep Ceira amused as her mother and grandmother waded through the mud collecting mussels. They'd feel for them with their bare feet then put their hand deep into the soft mud and pull out the shell.

They returned 20 minutes later with a 15 kilogram flour tin filled with about 30 kiwi-fruit-sized shells. I'd never seen them before and they reminded me of big fat scallops.

'We build a fire,' Leona announced. So together we gathered a pile of dry wood and lit a fire. I got the billy boiling, prepared the tea and laid out my spread. Once the fire had burnt down to smouldering ash, Leona scooped half the mussels out of the bag and dropped them into the warm embers. The heat quickly loosened the shells and she used a stick to pop them open.

'Here,' she said, passing me one. It looked like a big brown scallop but, to me, it tasted like a piece of old chewing gum with a chalky, muddy taste. I didn't want to offend her, and I gave it a darned good chew, but eventually I had to sheepishly admit defeat. Clearly mud mussels are an acquired taste! Fortunately Leona and her mother just laughed at my discomfort as I struggled to swallow it, until eventually I had to spit it into a tissue.

The men returned with three large catfish. I'd only ever seen catfish that were around a foot long, or about a third of a metre. These babies were just over a metre each – enormous. We admired the fish and then I offered around the scones and chocolate cake. Once everyone had eaten their fill, we wrapped the catfish in a piece of tarp, secured them to the roof rack and headed for home. I dropped the family off and drove back to my house with a big smile on my face. Despite the fact I'd been defeated by mozzies and found mud mussels were not my cup of tea, I'd had an absolute ball.

Back at work the following week, my mind turned to sex education. Ian had recently landed a second job helping out with admin at the local school and one day he introduced me to the school's counsellor, Ros. We hit it off straight away. A divorcee with a grown-up son and daughter, Ros had been living alone in Maningrida since 2008 and soon we began to meet up socially, sharing a cup of tea on each other's verandah, or a glass of wine over dinner.

'You should come and talk to the young girls at the school,' she said one day. 'I think you could really help with their sex education sessions.'

I thought this was a great idea. I'd been thinking of ways to develop relationships in the community outside the clinic and this would be an ideal opportunity to educate young women about birth control and perhaps stop unwanted pregnancies before they happened.

As well as dealing with all the prenatal and antenatal care in the community, it was my job to educate women about birth control and sexually transmitted infections (STIs). The most common form of contraception used in this community was Implanon, which comes in the form of a small soft rod that's implanted into the skin on the inner side of the upper arm and releases the birth control hormone progestogen. It's easy enough for a doctor to put it in and remove it with the help of a local anaesthetic, it lasts for three years and is 99 per cent effective.

However, obviously Implanon doesn't offer protection from STIs, and far too many young mothers I treated were testing positive to infections such as chlamydia and gonorrhoea. They took the condoms I offered them, but I wasn't convinced they were using them. I needed to find a way to get them to listen. Knowing what an important role fertility played in traditional culture, I tried pointing out that if a woman became infected with a sexually transmitted disease, her baby bag could become rotten and there'd be no babies. This did seem to work sometimes – at any rate, some mothers would suddenly take a lot more interest in learning how to use the condoms. But I felt I had a much better chance of getting my message across to the next generation by running classes at the school.

Like most adolescents, the students were very bashful about discussing sex, but not long after I'd started the classes a gaggle of giggling schoolgirls came to visit me at the clinic.

'Jasmine wants that Implanon,' one of them blurted out as the girl I presumed was Jasmine elbowed her in the ribs.

'And what about the rest of you?' I asked. More sniggers.

'We don't have boyfriends,' the tall girl answered.

'But what if you're out with a boy and he gets a twinkle in his eye?' I asked. 'If you have sex with that boy, a baby could grow in your stomach.'

The girls found it funny so I knew I'd broken the ice. And I knew it was important to make the connection between sex and babies, because some of them didn't necessarily understand this link.

'Come and see me again,' I told them. 'Whenever it's the right time you can come back with your mother, aunt or older sister.' As long as the relative or guardian they brought with them was over 18 and agreed to give their permission for a script, the girls were allowed the implant. I tried to emphasise that they must come back quickly if they started a sexual relationship – I always worried that by the time they did return there might be a baby on the go already.

One of Maningrida's best initiatives for new mothers was a playgroup called Families as First Teachers. It was run five days a week by a teacher called Michelle, and mothers with children up to the age of the four came along. The mothers were taught all kinds of things, from healthy nutrition for their babies and toddlers to art, typing and writing. As adult literacy levels in the community were low and most women had only limited schooling, this was a great opportunity for them to gain new skills as well. Meanwhile, the little ones got to play with fabulous toys and equipment to help their learning and developmental skills.

Michelle had been a teacher in the junior school before taking this job at the beginning of 2010 and there's no doubt that she transformed many women's lives. She was brilliant at helping to empower them to make positive choices for themselves and their children, and soon had some progressing to Certificates II and III in child care. She treated the women with a natural respect many may not have experienced before, and she had really won their trust.

After attending a few classes, I was so impressed that I asked if she'd be willing to help me host informal 'pop-up' antenatal classes at the playgroup. I explained that I'd like to talk to the women about things like childbirth and contraception, and try to improve their basic knowledge – there was only so much I could talk about when they came to the clinic for their check-ups.

Michelle agreed, so I began to give a morning talk at the playgroup every few weeks. To my relief, the women seemed receptive to what I had to say and word-of-mouth began to spread. Soon other new mums, and even pregnant siblings and relatives, were turning up to the classes.

You can imagine my surprise when one day I arrived to find a grinning Jo there, breastfeeding her three-month-old son, Alfred. Alfred had been born in Darwin the November before without any complications. Jo's initial dislike of me seemed to have been forgotten; now she was eager to share her new-found knowledge of childbirth.

'When the baby is ready to come out, sometimes the baby water breaks,' she announced to a group of teenagers as we talked about labour. 'Then the baby pains come; they come and go; then the big baby pain comes and that baby want to push out. That's when you push that baby out.'

Warming to her subject, she became very animated, crouching into different positions and huffing and puffing to demonstrate active labour – now speaking in language. The younger women looked on with amazement and some looked a little terrified – I think she frightened them a bit, but in a good way!

After that Jo became one of my most enthusiastic ambassadors in the community, joining me in the Troopie as I drove around the town picking up women from their homes and taking them to the clinic. 'Come on, let's get some food, clinic, medicine!' she'd sing out the window.

So, 10 months after arriving in Maningrida, I felt as though I'd finally nailed it, at least in the sense of building trust with the women in the community. At last it seemed that the women had overcome their wariness of me; they were even approaching me in the supermarket to tell me about an expectant mother I should see. The majority of the time I already had the woman on my list, but sometimes they gave me a new lead. All that mattered to me was that they trusted and wanted to confide in me like this. It was a wonderful feeling.

✳

We had only been at Maningrida for a few months when Lauren phoned to announce that she and her boyfriend, Brad, were going to be parents. When it came time for my granddaughter Eva's first birthday, Ian and I flew home to Wodonga to celebrate it, and spend some time with Lauren, who was by now 34 weeks pregnant.

She was blooming, with a sizeable baby bump. Of course, I asked to palpate her stomach, assuming the baby would be facing down, ready for birth; in fact, I could feel its head up near Lauren's ribcage.

When I told her I was pretty sure her baby was breech, Lauren immediately made an appointment with her midwife and was referred to an obstetrician. We'd just arrived back in Maningrida when she called to say she'd be having a caesarean two weeks later. The thought of being away from my daughter at that crucial time was too much: I immediately booked two weeks of personal leave and arranged to fly back to Wodonga the day after her caesarean.

Thankfully, her baby boy, Declan, arrived on 14 April with no complications, and, as promised, I arrived at the hospital the following day, eager to meet my new grandson. The moment I clapped eyes on this beautiful baby with his big brown eyes and little crop of thick dark hair I was smitten. For the next fortnight I spent time with Lauren and her family to help Lauren with breastfeeding and give her a break when she needed it while Brad was at work.

After such a blissful time bonding with my new grandson, I was very reluctant to return to Maningrida, but the great thing about modern technology is that I could still coo over all my grandchildren via Skype. One Sunday, after I'd been enjoying a relaxing hour talking to the girls on the webcam, I was called to the clinic – one of my patients was having pains.

'I'll be there in five,' I said. I knew Jane was about 34 weeks, just like Nina had been. When I got to the clinic, Jane was lying calmly on the bed and for a woman in labour, let alone early labour, she looking remarkably composed. She told me the pain had started at daylight. I alerted the doctor on call in Darwin and started Jane's basic observations – her temperature, pulse, blood pressure, blood sugar.

All was as it should be, and five minutes later CareFlight rang to say they had two planes on their way – one from Nhulunbuy, 600 kilometres to the east, which had a midwife on board; the other from Darwin, 500 kilometres to the west, which was carrying a pediatrician. Both would take an hour to get to Maningrida.

By now Jane was in established labour and was quietly coping with her contractions. She was about 6 centimetres dilated and had a very thin cervix, so once her contractions became stronger I knew her labour would progress quickly.

At that point a nurse arrived with the news that the plane from Darwin had been delayed. 'They're waiting for another nurse so we can evacuate a second patient who's got throat cancer – he's bleeding heavily.'

Jane was advancing rapidly and she was now growing agitated with each contraction. 'When will I go to Darwin?' she panted.

'You'll go with your baby,' I said, sounding as measured and reassuring as I could. I was pretty sure all would be well, but you just never know.

By now I'd been joined by a clinic doctor. Although she wasn't obstetric-trained, she'd be able to assist if Jane's baby needed to be resuscitated. Nevertheless, it was a huge relief when the CareFlight midwife, Fiona, finally bounded through the door. I explained how close Jane was to being fully dilated.

Half an hour later, the paediatrician arrived. We were all ready for the birth.

'Just listen to your body,' I urged Jane. 'When you get the urge, push your baby out.'

She immediately shuffled into a semi-sitting position on the bed. 'It's coming,' she cried, bearing down with gusto. Her pushes were effective and before long I could see the thin, transparent sac of her membranes. One contraction later they ruptured with a pop, spraying Fiona and me with clear amniotic fluid.

At this stage, I'd have expected to see the baby's head. Instead we got a nasty shock. All we could see were two little feet, with the cord sitting neatly between them. Fiona and I looked at each other in dismay. Not only was the baby breech, but we both knew that when the feet come first, there's a possibility the cervix isn't fully dilated, so its head can become stuck. In the hospital, there'd now be a mad rush to theatre for an emergency caesarean section, but we were of course hundreds of kilometres away from the nearest theatre.

Neither the clinic doctor nor the paediatrician had the experience to deal with this situation. It was down to Fiona and me to solve the problem.

I forced myself to be calm. Stirrups would have allowed the baby to hang with its head flexed as the head moved into the pelvis; it's important for the head to be flexed because it means it's the smallest diameter possible for birth. But we didn't have stirrips, so we had to reverse Jane's position. We asked her to get onto all fours. This was the first time I'd facilitated a breech birth and now I had to think upside down.

Fiona and I knew that for a breech baby to move smoothly through the birth canal, the baby's back must be uppermost so the head is fully flexed for birth. At this point the baby had been born up to her belly and her heels were pointing to the ceiling: the positioning was all wrong.

'The baby's facing the wrong way,' I said to Fiona. 'We've got to rotate her.'

Gently holding onto the baby's tiny pelvis, I carefully coaxed her little body around to face the other way. I manoeuvred her arms out so they weren't taking up space in Jane's pelvis. Jane stayed in brilliant control, doing exactly as we asked, while we slowly manoevred the baby out.

Then, when instructed, she pushed and, bingo, a baby girl with masses of black curly hair slid into my hands. Her placenta slipped out in hot pursuit, so it looked for a second as if she were wearing it as a hat. Then there came the sound of a hearty cry. Fiona and I smiled shakily. I have to admit that I almost felt like bursting into tears with relief. We both took a few deep breaths to quell our nerves and congratulated each other.

Despite weighing just 2 kilograms, the biggest relief for all of us was that Jane's baby seemed in good condition, flexing her tiny little muscles and crying with good strong breaths.

I thanked Fiona profusely for her help – I wasn't sure what I'd have done without her, helping me work out how to handle such a tricky and potentially life-threatening situation.

Remarkably, a smiling Jane seemed oblivious to the acute emergency that had just unfolded in the birthing room. After being checked by the paediatrician, her little girl was placed into an isolette on an ambulance trolley and mother and daughter were transferred to the airport for their journey to Darwin.

As my colleagues headed home to enjoy the last of the Sunday evening light, Ian joined me at the clinic to help mop the floor while I bleached, changed the linen and restocked the room, ready for the next emergency birth!

With a sense of weary satisfaction, we headed home for a celebratory glass of wine on the verandah. Despite the initial terror I'd felt when I saw those feet, delivering a breech baby had given me a huge confidence boost – and it was good to know I could keep a cool head in a real crisis when there was no backup to save the day.

Jane returned to the community with her bouncing baby, Markisha, a couple of weeks later and I was thrilled to catch up with her at the clinic.

'Did you know we were worried about getting her out?' I asked Jane.

'No,' she smiled. 'I thought everybody had babies like that.' Sometimes ignorance really is bliss!

Chapter 14
Shockwaves

Just when I thought I had overcome my fear of the slavering packs of camp dogs roaming the neighbourhood, I was shocked back to reality. While enjoying a quiet natter on the verandah with my friend Ros one Sunday afternoon, our peace was shattered by high-pitched squeals from the house next door. Eventually we saw the source of the terrified squeaks – a puppy had wedged his head in my neighbour's gate and was desperately trying to struggle free.

Ros sped down the steps to rescue him but as she crouched down to free the little chap, without warning a pack of five growling dogs came racing around the corner.

'Ros! Watch out!' I yelled. It was too late. In a split second
the pack had knocked her to the ground and one had sunk its
teeth into her leg. Hearing my horrified shrieks, Ian rushed
to the door and grabbed the dog stick as Ros began to scream
for help. He charged over to her, scattered the pack with the
stick and his shouts, and yanked the dog that was still on her
by its tail. It retreated with a startled yelp.

I'd been frozen with fear, but now I rushed down to poor
Ros and with the help of another neighbour gently lifted her
up and took her into the house. Her face was a ghastly shade
of grey, she was trembling badly and could hardly speak. No
wonder – the dog had savaged her horribly. She had a huge
gash on her left calf, bleeding teeth marks all up her back and
puncture marks on her left shoulder.

Looking back, I think we were all in shock, so I can't
imagine how Ros must have felt – she was ashen with fear
and pain as we examined her as carefully as we could.

Anxious to get Ros's wounds cleaned and treated as soon
as possible, and to get something for the pain and shock, we
helped her into the car and I drove her to the clinic. Pam, a
newbie nurse who'd just come up from New South Wales,
was on duty and she couldn't hide her astonishment that a
town dog would be so aggressive and do this much damage.
I remembered how a couple of years earlier I'd been the same,
hardly able to imagine that one of the biggest dangers I'd
have to face was from the local dog population.

Pam disinfected and bandaged Ros's lesions, and stitched
a deeper wound on her calf, as well as giving her a tetanus

booster jab. She suggested we call Darwin so Ros could be observed for 24 hours in a hospital. By the time I'd driven her home and helped her to gather some clean clothes and toiletries for the trip, we'd got the message that she'd have to wait until tomorrow morning to be transferred. I insisted she stay the night with us. Dosed up to the eyeballs on heavy painkillers, she seemed to drift off quickly once she was in our spare bed, and when I checked on her in the night she was out for the count.

While Ros put on a brave face, the next morning the pain was clearly very bad and she was valiantly fighting back tears, still traumatised by the horrible savagery and suddenness of the attack. When Ian and I waved her off at lunchtime, I hoped she'd not come back to the community until she was feeling stronger.

When she called five days later she sounded much more like herself. 'You can tell Pam she did an excellent job,' she told me. 'The doctor says it is a nasty wound but I won't need any surgery.'

Ros spent six days in Darwin Hospital, on a course of strong antibiotics, and then returned to her home in Queensland for 10 weeks to recuperate. Meanwhile, Ian had been busy helping the police to identify the offending dog, as it would have to be put down. There was no way we could risk anyone else being attacked so badly, or worse. And we all would feel a lot safer knowing the offender was gone.

However, in Aboriginal culture you should not kill a dog, unless it gives you permission to do so, and you need to summon a 'dog dreaming man' to determine this. Even before Ros's attack, there'd been growing concern about the large number of camp dogs in the community and the West Arnhem Shire Council had wanted to do a cull. But after consulting the community, it had never happened because at the time the dog dreaming man couldn't be reached – he lived in another town.

In this case, though, the dog was clearly a danger, so the police intervened and, in consultation with the family, the culprit was taken care of.

'The family seemed to accept what their dog had done,' Ian said. 'The police just took him.'

True to her word, Ros returned 10 weeks later. She had a scarred left calf, but her psychological wounds appeared to have healed, and she was resolved to stay in Maningrida.

Understandably, though, she remained very wary of dogs. And she was not the only one. After that I made doubly sure never to go anywhere without a stick, or two!

When my sister Faye and brother-in-law Paul decided to come and visit us, Ian and I were looking forward to seeing them and showing them our new life.

Perhaps I should have thought a little bit more about the culture shock I'd had when I'd first arrived, but I guess after being in Maningrida for more than two years, Ian and I were used to the sights and sounds and no longer saw it from the perspective of newcomer. So I was completely unprepared for the looks on Paul and Faye's faces when I showed them the town. As we drove around, I was reminded that my sister and I had grown into very different people.

Like most people, Faye enjoyed her comforts and being close to her friends and in a place she knew well. Maningrida was a huge leap into the unknown. For her, the contrast was a little more than culture shock. Although she'd been curious about my new life and eager to visit, once she saw it she made no bones about how she felt. She told me point-blank that she could never live here – in what she called a 'rubbish tip'!

Faye and Paul's life on a farm in country Victoria could not have been more different to ours in Maningrida, and they were horrified at the litter on the streets, the camp dogs everywhere, and the unmaintained buildings that made up the town.

Shocked at her response, I was nevertheless surprised by how quickly and strongly I leapt to the defence of my new life and home – it made me realise how much both Ian and I loved and felt part of the community here.

But when I'd recovered my equilibrium and thought about it, I felt less outraged about their reactions – I could see their first impressions in the context of my first visit, how I had felt I was in a different world. It was so removed and alien compared to their home and their way of life. And, after all, they'd only seen the very surface of things.

Funnily enough, it was not until Faye and Paul were heading back home that they caught a glimpse of why we loved our new stomping ground – and began to see for themselves how unique and beautiful it is. Setting out to drive them back to Darwin, we discovered we were one of the first vehicles to make the journey following a very wet season, so getting through the first river out of Maningrida proved tricky.

After surveying the swell, Ian suggested we cross a little further along in case the force of the current tipped over our car. I got out, peeled off my leggings and walked thigh-deep into the water to guide him through. Then I watched, wincing, as the car rocked up the bank and through a narrow gap between two trees, scraping the side mirrors in the process.

'Only eighteen more crossings to go!' I laughed.

Despite the challenges of getting through, Faye and Paul were delighted by the lush outback scenery and all the birdlife around us, and we could see that they were falling for the beauty of our surroundings just as we had in our first wet season.

But their initial response to the rudimentary nature of our everyday life in Maningrida did make me realise that I no longer saw the bush conditions I lived in as I had when I'd first arrived. I didn't see our house or our environment as alien or strange, or lacking in the things I needed. It had become home and it was as simple as that.

I realised that I'd grown accustomed to our life in Maningrida as perhaps others never would – and how fortunate I'd been that Ian and I had been open to this adventure and were able to adapt as we had.

One thing I was also sure of was that I would not have been able to do it without him by my side. Like all couples, we'd had our ups and downs, but they had only brought us closer and we made a great team.

✳

Since accompanying Leona and her mother on their mud mussels expedition, I had been eager to learn more about traditional fishing and hunting, and, depending on the mozzies, perhaps even try my hand at catching something myself!

The Aboriginal population of Arnhem Land has always relied on the land and the sea for its food supply, and their traditional methods of hunting and gathering have been passed from generation to generation. Although many animals, plants and flowers in the region are now classified as protected species, the local people have special privileges to hunt and gather there.

Turtles are a good example. There are seven species of sea turtle in the world, and six of them live in the waters of the Northern Territory: the Flatback, Green, Hawksbill, Loggerhead, Olive Ridley and Leatherback. Both the federal and Northern Territory state governments protect all six species, but because these marine turtles are culturally important to Aboriginals from this area, and are still often used for food and in some of their ceremonies, local Aboriginals are permitted to hunt the creatures, as long as they do so in their own country and not for commercial gain. Nor must the creatures be hunted to the extent of 'unsustainable harvest', but there is little danger of that as the traditional owners of the land are experts at ensuring their food sources follow their natural circle of life in the wild. We could all learn a thing or two from their ability to live off and respect the land.

Occasionally when I was at the coast, I'd see Aboriginal men standing in boats clutching long spears to hunt Green turtles. On another expedition, I was lucky enough to watch some of the locals as they hunted long-neck turtles in the fresh water, wading in ankle-deep and poking expertly around in the mud until they found one.

I was even given the opportunity to taste some turtle meat. The turtle is cooked on a fire, and the neck, which is a bit like a chicken's – with lots of small bones – is eaten first. When I first tried it, I must admit all I could really taste was charcoal, but the flavour of the meat is often compared to chicken, and it's considered a delicacy. It's also an invaluable source of protein and plays an important role in some traditional ceremonies.

Once the shell's been stripped of the meat, some artists in the community use them as canvases on which to paint fine-lined paintings of crocodiles, barramundi, or turtles, in traditional colours such as tan, black and white. To acquire one, you need a proof of purchase as authentication that the shell has not been poached.

One form of hunting and gathering I didn't want any part of was raiding crocodile nests for eggs. This is conservation-based work: local Aboriginal rangers employed by the Department of Environment for their skills and local knowledge regularly risk their lives raiding crocodile nests in the boggy wetlands to collect the eggs so they can be incubated and hatched in a controlled environment. The week-old hatchlings are sold to the crocodile farms in Darwin, where they grow and eventually become part of the industry for croc meat and skins.

Crocodiles construct their huge nests from sticks or long grass, piling these into a mound to keep the eggs above the water and safe from flooding. The average nest can contain up to 70 eggs and each egg can weigh up to 110 grams or more, and measure 80 by 50 millimetres. Rangers spot them from their boats or a helicopter. If they're in a helicopter, they throw down pink ribbon, of all things, to mark the location of the nest; the air from the rotor blades forces the ribbon to swirl down to where the nest is. That's when the fun really begins.

Luckily we didn't have to join the rangers to know how dangerous their work was. Pam's husband Glenn, who was one of the local support team that helps out on the hunts – driving speed boats, helping net mud crab, fishing barramundi for bait – regaled us with stories of how they struck a nest.

'We go in with huge oars and bash the water and ground around the nest to see if the croc is there,' he said. 'If we don't get chased by an angry mother, we go and grab the eggs. The rule is, the bigger the nest, the bigger the croc.'

Once the eggs are safely collected, each one is carefully marked and packed up in an esky in exactly the same position it was found in: if it is moved and stored the wrong way up, the baby crocs will most likely drown in the yolk. The eggs are kept in incubators for up to 90 days, or until the big moment when the little tackers hatch.

After enthralling us with his stories of the rangers' derring-do, Glenn invited me to visit to see the baby crocodiles coming out of their shells. Well, that was an offer I wasn't going to refuse! There was no way I wanted to join a raiding party on a mama crocodile's nest, but a chance to help little croc babies come into the world was too good to pass up. So a few weeks later I found myself at the rangers' station, carefully peeling away the shell of a cracked crocodile egg. As I pulled off the top layer of shell, out popped a little green slimy head with open jaws, and a long body with a cute little pot belly.

'They come out very well-nourished,' Glenn explained. 'They don't need to be fed for a week because their bellies are full of yolk.'

'Never smile at a crocodile,' I laughed as the little fella scrambled out onto my hand and we eyeballed each other. It's not every day you get to birth a baby croc!

*

We'd become good friends with Pam and Glenn, so the next time Nina and her family invited us for a weekend 'out bush', we asked them if our two friends could come along. Nina was happy to include them on an expedition to a peaceful spot a little way out of town, where we set up camp among long savannah grass and gnarly gum trees.

Ian and I took our mossie dome tent – with a mesh at the top instead of canvas – as we loved sleeping with the stars in full view. Nina and her family slept on blankets on the soft sand on the flat of the river. She made sure we were settled not too far away from them, up on a bank, further away from the water – she was very protective of us, ensuring we felt safe in these new surroundings, which were so dear to her and her family. This was Nina's mother's country and she told us they'd come out here for as long as she could remember.

While Ian and Glenn headed off to fish for barramundi with Nina's husband Chris, Nina, Pam and I relaxed by the river's edge – it was beautiful fresh water and clear as crystal.

When Krystal and Kurt bounded in, I looked at Nina with concern. Wasn't she worried about crocs?

'We swim here, Pet – no crocs. Come!' Krystal laughed. She gestured for us to jump in.

'It's true,' said Nina, and she too plunged into the river with a giggling Carla and wide-eyed Charles on her hips.

Gingerly, Pam and I removed our shoes and lowered ourselves into the water. At least we'd see it coming, I thought, trying to suppress my anxiety. But once I'd got over my apprehension, I happily succumbed to the peaceful serenity of the water and our surroundings. It was such a magical, peaceful spot and it was such a generous gift for Nina to

share her mother's country, part of her family for generations, with us. We were literally surrounded by beauty. There
was no pollution and no rubbish – just everything as nature
had intended.

After our dip, Nina, Pam and I spent a lazy afternoon
sipping tea brewed in the billy over an open fire and chatting
as the children played chasing games around the trees and
dived into the water. As little Carla climbed on to my lap for
a cuddle, Pam and I listened, enthralled, while Nina told us
some of the traditional Aboriginal stories – including one
about a terrifying character who sings people to their deaths.

'There is a sorcerer man who sings people. He comes
to them as they sleep and sings them through the window.
Nobody sees him or knows who it is. He follows the person
around without being seen and sings them to commit suicide.
The sorcerer is constantly around watching but nobody
knows who he is.'

Nina explained that the sorcerer would carry out his
singing on someone, and he or she would then become ill.
He would be present when the body was found, with the
mourning family, at the airport when the body is flown out
and back to the community, at the funeral and the burial.

As the sun began to set, the men returned with six big
barramundi, which we cooked on the hot coals. It was so
fleshy and delicious, and tasted better than any fish I'd ever
had before. The sky flushed red as hundreds of birds – brolgas,
storks and magpie geese – flew across it, their silhouettes
illuminated against the beautiful sunset.

'This is incredible,' I whispered to Ian later as we snuggled up in sleeping bags, gazing at the constellations above us from our tent. We listened to the soft bush lullaby of frogs, owls and kingfisher birds, and I was lulled into a deep sleep, utterly content, at peace with the world and in awe of the whole experience.

A few weeks after our trip with Nina, I drove out with a nurse from the clinic – another Ian – on an outstation visit. The purpose of these visits was to provide the facilities and expertise of the health service to the people who'd chosen to live 'on country' rather than in the town, and we made them regularly during the dry season. These trips were impossible, however, during the wet unless an emergency cropped up, in which case the flying doctors would go in. Each outstation had a satellite phone for incoming calls and emergency 000 outgoing calls only.

I went out on this particular visit because I wanted to check on a pregnant woman I knew was living at the out-station, about an hour out of Maningrida. But since I was there, of course I helped Ian with other general checks for anyone who wanted or needed them.

After we'd completed these and I'd done my checks on the mother-to-be, we had time to spare before we packed up, so I offered to talk 'women's business'. There were a few nods among those present, with all eyes darting to an older woman, who was sitting cross-legged on a mat on the verandah of the nearest house.

As is customary, I introduced myself to her first and paid my respects. The elder in Aboriginal tradition is the highly respected head of the family, the person who instils knowledge, provides guidance and conducts ceremonies within a family or community. It was necessary and culturally respectful for me to address her first. But while she smiled welcomingly at me, the elder didn't seem to understand what I was saying. Eventually a middle-aged woman from the group began to translate for her, and through my local interpreter it was agreed that we could indeed discuss women's business. Shuffling to her feet, the elder beckoned me to follow her into a tin shelter away from the house.

There, six women aged from about 15 to 50 joined us as we sat in a circle on the floor.

After introducing myself, I offered contraceptive advice, tried to explain as clearly as I could the importance of having a PAP smear and explained the advantages of some general health checks that they might think about having, now or down the line. I also explained that I was always available at the clinic in Maningrida if they wanted a private discussion. Then I asked if there were any questions.

No one said a word.

'Contraception? Trouble with period? Tummy pain?' I asked through my trusty local interpreter, thinking ruefully that my list of ailments sounded a bit like an advertisement.

No one seemed keen to volunteer any information. I noticed that one of the teenage girls, who can't have been more than 15, had her eyes to the floor. I wondered if she was pregnant.

'Are there any babies coming?' I asked tentatively.

'They're good girls,' a woman in her forties said immediately. 'They don't need anything.'

And that was the end of women's business. I felt a little dismayed I couldn't talk to or offer any help to anyone, especially this young girl, but of course they didn't know me and they had every right to guard their privacy.

'I'm at the clinic in Maningrida every day,' I told them again as I stood up to leave. 'If you want to talk, come and see me. Just ask for Beth, the midwife.'

Around eight months later this same young girl – just 15 – was brought to me by two older women. She was 35 weeks pregnant and in early labour – they told me she'd been paining in the night. Fortunately we were able to get her to Darwin in time, and I was later told she'd had a healthy boy and all had been well.

Our next stop was an outstation in which a small community of 40 Aboriginals lived on ancestral land. We parked outside an abandoned schoolhouse but, apart from having to brandish our trusty dog sticks to shoo away the inevitable pack of barking dogs, the place seemed pretty deserted. Just when we were beginning to think we'd wasted a visit, a sleepy-looking elderly man meandered out of a house, scratching his head and blinking in the sunlight.

'Where would you like us to start the clinic?' Ian asked. He'd telephoned ahead to say we were coming, so people who needed to be seen knew to bring us their medication if they needed more, or to come and find us.

He pointed to the schoolhouse. We set up a folding table, six folding chairs and a large container of cool water beside the building, then laid out instruments for checking blood pressure, blood sugar, temperature, ear health and haemoglobin. Our car fridge contained injectable penicillin and immunisations, along with containers for various types of pathology tests.

By now people were shuffling out of the houses near the schoolhouse and starting to line up. Between us, Ian and I checked each patient's history and determined whether blood samples should be taken for pathology – the people we saw were given routine annual adult health checks to determine their kidney and liver function, blood sugar levels and cholesterol, as well as general blood tests.

All the while I kept my eyes peeled for suspected baby bumps – I knew that at least one pregnant woman lived in the community.

'Is Tabitha here?' I asked one of the women.

'She's sleeping,' she replied, but after some gentle prompting, she agreed to go and find her. Ten minutes later I saw a slight but clearly pregnant woman walking towards our table. She had two small children with her, clinging shyly to her legs. As I took her blood pressure we chatted about how she was feeling, her previous pregnancies and her general health.

'I'm healthy girl,' she told me, beaming. She certainly had beautiful white teeth. So many of the women in my care had rotten teeth due to poor diet and a lack of tooth-brushing, but living off the land and eating bush tucker was clearly working for Tabitha.

I asked if I could check her baby's heartbeat and growth, and she pointed to a small, disused shelter where we could do that. Of course, it had no white sheets or padded pillows, just bare concrete with tufts of grass growing from cracks in the floor. But Tabitha was unperturbed and she lay down and lifted her top. As we both heard the baby's heartbeat on my Doppler, I was rewarded with another flash of her perfect smile.

Back at the makeshift clinic I examined Tabitha's two children, looking into their ears and throats, recording their weights and carrying out fingerpick tests to check for anaemia. They were both healthy and thriving.

I asked Tabitha if she could get a member of her family to bring her to Maningrida for a scan the following Tuesday, when the ultrasound team was coming from Darwin for the day. She said she would and, true to her word, she was first to arrive at the clinic on Tuesday morning. We confirmed that she was 20 weeks pregnant, with a healthy-looking baby, and I asked her to return the following month.

I didn't see or hear from her after that, but 10 weeks later a 000 call came through to the clinic. I was on leave at the time, but the manager was told Tabitha had gone into premature labour – at only 30 weeks pregnant. The timing couldn't have been worse because by now the roads to the outstations had become impassable as the rivers were running perilously high.

The clinic team swung into action and arranged for a local small aircraft and another midwife to fly to the outstation to assess the situation and report back via satellite phone. Once they'd done this, the CareFlight team was dispatched for an emergency evacuation. Thankfully Tabitha was flown out in time, and gave birth in Darwin the same day. I was relieved to hear later that her small baby had survived and seemed to be doing well.

After several weeks in Darwin, Tabitha and her little girl returned to the outstation. I was thrilled to see on my next visit there that she had a plump, happy baby nursing on her breast. It was such a good outcome when I thought of what could have happened.

So much can go wrong with births at the best of times. In these remote areas we had to plan ahead for risks and complications that in a town or city environment, where sophisticated equipment and highly trained medics are minutes away, could be dealt with immediately. Here, good luck and timing seemed to play as much a part in the survival of early babies or the smooth running of complicated labours as did our expertise. If the plane hadn't reached Tabitha in time, her premature baby might not have made it.

As the wet season arrived in a flash of thunderous clouds and torrential downpours, Ian and I flew to Darwin for a short holiday with Lauren, Clare and their babies. It was wonderful to catch up with the girls and their growing families as we wandered around the city and visited the lions, tigers and crocodiles at Crocadylus Park, billed as 'Darwin's premier tourist attraction', and home to 1000 crocodiles. You'd think we would have had enough of those in our part of the world, but I felt a lot safer seeing them in captivity, and couldn't help wondering how many of them had been born at Maningrida.

As always, it was hard to say goodbye to our daughters and grandchildren. While I loved the new life Ian and I had carved out and wouldn't swap our adventures in the outback for anything, having to part ways with my family was definitely a wrench sometimes.

Life soon returned to normal and by the time Ian and I flew home again that December to spend the holidays with Clare and Lauren in Wodonga, I felt a lot more settled and resigned to the fact that I'd always miss my family, no matter where I was. And this year we had the added pleasure of two grandchildren to keep us entertained.

We were halfway through a lazy Boxing Day, grazing on Christmas leftovers and watching the kids play in the backyard, when I received a devastating call from Michelle. Nina's daughter Carla had died. She had choked on a sausage on Christmas Day.

When someone passes away in an Aboriginal community, it is culturally inappropriate and disrespectful to refer to that person by their name, so from then on we referred to this dear little girl indirectly. As tears streamed down my cheeks, Michelle from Families as First Teachers gently explained how everyone had worked so hard to try to resuscitate Nina's darling child, but to no avail.

I just could not believe what I was hearing – it was unthinkable that this lively, beautiful little girl was gone. I could hardly bear to imagine how Nina and her family must be feeling. And the others – had they seen their sister struggling for breath? My mind was going at a hundred miles a minute and as a mother myself I couldn't help thinking how broken with grief Nina must be.

Wiping away my tears, I did my best to compose myself, then I dialled Nina's number.

'Pam tried really hard to save her, Pet,' Nina told me as she let out heartbroken sobs. It was absolutely devastating to hear her beside herself with grief and to think she had lost her beloved daughter in such a cruel way.

That night at home none of us said much – we couldn't get over the news of the tragedy. Like me, Ian was devastated. We just could not imagine that lovely little baby we'd grown to love was gone. She was just a few months apart in age from our granddaughter.

Later, Pam told me the call had come through just after they'd finished their Christmas lunch. Everyone had rushed to the clinic to help and doctors from the emergency department at the Royal Darwin Hospital had directed treatment by video, glued to the screen, as the team in Maningrida worked desperately to bring her back to life, increasingly in despair as it became clear there was nothing anyone could do to save her. Now her little body was on its way to Darwin for a post-mortem.

When I got back to the community a fortnight later, the first thing I did was call on Nina. She told me there had been sorry business all week and that her darling baby's body had come back to the town the week before. She asked if I would come to the funeral.

The next day I made my way to the burial spot close to Nina's home, where ceremonial dancing and music would lead her daughter on her journey to be laid to rest. A crowd of at least 150 people had gathered by the time a minister began to speak in language. While I could only pick up a few words, I was deeply moved by the intensity of the mourners' grief for this little girl and her family.

As Nina and her female relatives began to cry and wail, I couldn't hold back my own sorrow. And when I saw Nina's sister was holding a machete to inflict some sorry cuts on herself, I turned my head, unable to watch.

Two days later I went to see Nina. We embraced silently and held each other for a long time, heaving with sobs. Then she showed me all the flowers the family had received, and we visited her baby's grave, which lay under the shade of a large tree. The tiny burial spot was covered with pretty artificial flowers and my heart broke all over again. For some time we stood arm in arm, each deep in our thoughts.

A month after her daughter's funeral, Nina came to see me at the clinic. 'I want to take this out,' she said, pointing to the contraceptive implant in her arm. 'I want another baby.'

I wondered if she was ready, and we talked about her waiting a little longer to make certain. Although she agreed, three weeks later she came back and asked again for the implant to be removed.

Two months later Nina was pregnant, and she ended up giving birth to a baby girl. She named her Carla.

Chapter 15
Hunting and gathering

One day as I was leaving work I found a woman in her sixties sitting cross-legged outside the clinic. She told me her name was Esther, and when I asked her if she needed a lift home, she happily accepted my offer and said she'd show me where she lived. She made herself comfortable in the passenger seat and I introduced myself as the midwife at the clinic.

Esther had such a happy smile. I asked her what she did.

'I do weaving. Baskets, mats, dillybag,' she told me with a big grin. 'But I need car to get pandanus.'

I asked her where she got them.

'First Creek, plenty mob there. Not far.' I worked out that meant there was a lot of pandanus there and it wasn't far out of town. By now we'd come to her house, and as I pulled over she asked if I'd take her to First Creek.

I told her I'd happily take her at the weekend. And so my friendship began with dear sweet Esther.

On Saturday morning I rolled up to Esther's house as agreed and she climbed into my car with her stick, a long, thin piece of wood with a hook on the end. She directed me to another house, where a thin lady with grey woolly hair clambered into the Nissan Patrol. She introduced herself as Sheila; I later discovered from a nurse at the clinic that she was an Arnhem Land artist renowned for weaving beautiful floor mats and dillybags. The floor mats had concentric circles of different colours – red, yellow, black, white, dark grey – that became bigger and bigger as the mat did. She would then leave long bushy strands floating free and fanning outwards, so that the mat ended up looking like a brightly coloured sun with scores of rays shining out. They were exquisitely beautiful objects, striking and of course entirely formed from nature, being constructed from scratch with the pandanus.

We also took with us that day Martha, a stout elder with grey wiry hair, and another weaver called Nancy. They were all holding large postbags, which I assumed were for carrying their harvest.

Off we set off towards the bush, with Esther as navigator. As I drove, there was much laughter from the ladies. I didn't understand what they were saying but I could tell they were happy to be off to gather pandanus, and no doubt to have such a willing chauffeur.

Soon after, Esther told me to turn left and about 10 kilometres down the road she told me to stop at a small concrete bridge. The women piled out of the car. Clutching her stick, Esther headed for a big tree that looked a bit like a palm but had thinner reeds growing in a spiral at the top of its trunk – like a pineapple on a tall stalk. With her stick she dragged the innermost leaves of the tree down towards her, and, seemingly unconcerned by the thin spikes protruding from their sides, effortlessly broke them off with her bare hands, with a cracking noise. The other women helped, and in next to no time they'd gathered a pile of pandanus, and had filled all their postbags.

'We go to Rocky Point,' Esther announced when they'd finished.

I didn't know how much further Rocky Point was and I didn't have much fuel left, so I suggested we went back to the bridge and had a cup of tea and some scones I'd packed for our outing. The women built a fire, I boiled the billy, and my scones were devoured with enthusiasm. Refreshed, we secured the pandanus and a pile of wood on the roof rack and headed back to town. But about 5 kilometres out of Maningrida, Esther asked me to stop again.

When I asked her why, she said, 'We get colour. You got spade?'

I unscrewed the shovel on the roof rack for Esther and all four ladies headed into the scrub, with me following, keen to learn what the source of this colour would be and how they would collect it. Stopping at what looked to me like ordinary reedy grasses, they explained that the red they liked to use in their weaving came from the bulb from which these grasses grew. First, the women dug out the bulb from the ground, like you would a potato. They explained that you have to be careful the bulbs don't snap off when you're trying to pull them out.

Next, they went off to find the yellow dye they needed. This was extracted from the roots of a shrub that I now know is called *Coelospermum reticulatum*. Once the women had found the right bush, they dug up as much of the root as they could, alternating with the digging and working up quite a sweat. When they'd removed enough soil, they got right down on the ground and used their bare hands to scoop it away to expose the root properly. I took my turn and found it back-breaking work, although the soil was sandy and, at first, easy to dig.

Back in town, I stopped to help unload some of the pandanus, dye and root at each of the women's houses. I was fascinated to see what they'd make with them, and they promised they'd show me.

The next day, I took Ian to meet Esther. We found her sitting on her verandah, dividing the pandanus leaves into thin lengths, and stripping off the spikes, ready to boil with the colours they'd collected. The women used the dyes and pandanus as soon as possible after they'd gathered them, because the dried strips get harder to work with the longer they're stored, and the roots and bulbs dry up quickly.

Esther's daughter Christine was busy boiling the bulbs in flour drums of water to extract the red colour. The roots from the *Coelospermum* were chopped up into small shards and put into a separate drum. There was also a black dye Christine had created using leaves from another tree.

When the batches of colour were ready, Esther boiled some strips of reed with the red, some with the yellow and the rest with the black, then left them to dry on the verandah in the sun.

'Tomorrow I weave,' she said.

The following day I returned to watch as she wove the strips of red, yellow and black into a basket. The basket she was making had a very tight circle in the middle at the bottom. She was using long strands of natural pandanus (dried but not coloured), and working them round and round, then weaving the coloured strips over, so the natural strips were hidden. The basket soon started to take shape as she twisted and tied and began to build the sides with her nimble fingers. Then she'd weave another colour in to make stripes. It reminded me a little of the macramé classes I had done back in the 1970s but the results were much more beautiful!

Sitting cross-legged, she worked with a determined concentration, even using her toes – she held the long strands of the pandanus between her big and second toe like an extra hand. She made it look effortless, such was her speed and skill, but I could see it was extremely intricate work. I was amazed, not only by her skill but by her stamina – she didn't once take a break or get up to stretch out her legs. I know

I wouldn't have lasted five minutes sitting on that concrete verandah, and there was no way I'd have been able to weave even a couple of the strands together, with either my hands or feet!

We chatted as her fingers kept working, her peering at me through her unruly white hair. She told me her mother taught her weaving, and she'd taught Christine. They sold their work in the Art Centre that had been built in Maningrida since I'd been living there, which had a website so the craft could be on-sold; the centre also featured the work at many of the Indigenous arts festivals in Darwin.

Two weeks later, Esther's friend Sheila asked me to drive her and two other women to a local hunting spot called Crab Creek, a mangrove-lined tidal area on the edge of the bush. When we got there, I watched as the women headed onto the moist, muddy sand to collect small, spiral-shaped shellfish, which were referred to as 'long bum' because of their shape.

'Pet, you come with me,' Sheila said. I followed as she took a different direction up a sandbank, following the tidal stream. Clutching a stick, she kept her eyes peeled to the ground until she spotted a watery hole in the sand. I noticed there were some scratchings around the edge and wondered if that was what had caught her eye. Plonking down cross-legged on the moist sand, Sheila took her stick and poked it in the hole. Almost immediately I heard a clunk.

'There's one in here!' she said, smiling up at me.

Within seconds, she'd used her stick to coax out a dinner-plate-sized crab. She held it down firmly with her stick. The crab fought back, snapping its two-inch claws, but it was no match for Sheila. Fearlessly she grabbed a pincer and snapped it clean off. Within seconds the other claw was gone too and she placed the crab and the claws in her bag. A few steps further along the sand Sheila found her next victim and it too was deposited into the bag. Sheila's energy was unbelievable. For 45 minutes she worked tirelessly, pulling in an impressive haul of around 30 crabs.

Back at the car the other women had gathered a veritable harvest of long bums.

Next, Sheila directed me to Rocky Point. It turned out to be a beautiful beach, surrounded by distinctive rock formations, which looked out to the Arafura Sea and north to New Guinea. As we walked along the pristine sand, we gathered wood until we found the perfect spot under the shade of a tree to build a fire. Sheila handed me a bucket.

'Get me water,' she said. (There are no unnecessary pleasantries like please and thank you in Aboriginal speech, so of course Sheila didn't use them in English either.)

I couldn't help thinking of all those stories of unsuspecting tourists being grabbed by crocodiles while they loitered at the water's edge, so I kept my eyes peeled for any movement as I collected the water to cook the crabs in. A hungry crocodile can come from nowhere surprisingly quickly.

I made it back to the campfire intact, and boiled the billy to make tea as Sheila put a feast of long bums on the white-hot coals. Almost immediately the tops of the shells started to froth – the flesh I could see reminded me of luminous green oysters.

Pulling them out of the fire after a few minutes, Sheila's friends cracked the spiral shells on a rock and then pulled open the crushed hulls to extract the meat, which, now it was cooked, had changed to a grey colour. They asked if I'd like to try some and of course I said yes. They were absolutely delicious – they tasted a bit like sweet oysters.

Meanwhile, Sheila threw a couple of crabs into the bucket of boiling water and let them cook for 15 minutes.

Once they'd turned red and she was satisfied they were cooked, she asked me to get a bucket of cold water in which to cool them. When they were ready to eat she offered me some, but I'd seen how hard they'd worked for them so I told the women my husband could go fishing for my crabs and this was for them. I knew they didn't get to do this very often.

That day out marked the beginning of a very special friendship between Sheila and me, and afterwards I often accompanied her hunting and gathering at the weekends. I loved being in her company. She was so kind and patient with me and so calm and accepting. I also loved watching her work, both gathering the pandanus and hunting crabs with a stick. Her movements were so graceful and fluid, and she had incredible endurance and strength. So it came as a great shock to discover she was battling cancer.

'I had it before,' she said calmly. 'In my breast. They took it away.'

A month or so later, Sheila told me she needed treatment for endometrial cancer and would have to go to Darwin to undergo surgery. Before she left she showed me a beautiful dillybag she'd just finished. It was red, charcoal-coloured and a golden yellow, with a flat base and a natural string handle to hold on your shoulder. The string was made from the bark of a tree, which the women rolled on their legs until it looked like string. I'd never seen them do it, but Sheila told me it left their legs hairless.

She pointed at the bag and said, 'I made it for you.'

I was so touched. 'You can't give it to me!' I protested. 'It's too much!' I knew her work was in demand at the Art Centre, where she'd be paid for it. But she insisted.

A few weeks later I was sitting on the verandah when I spotted her coming along the road with a walking stick. I was so thrilled that I ran down the steps to meet her. 'Come and sit with me. I'll make tea.'

'How are you feeling after the operation?' I asked once I'd got her seated on a comfy chair.

'Not too crook,' she said. 'The doctor fellas in Darwin say I need radiation.'

That didn't sound good but I didn't like to probe too much, so the two of us sat there quietly sipping our tea and listening to the sounds of the town.

✻

By now both our daughters were pregnant again and Lauren's due date was approaching fast. She was having an elective caesarean, so I booked some time off to be there to meet her beautiful little girl, Layla, straight after she was born.

Lauren was a force to be reckoned with after the birth, though – it was as if she hadn't had a big operation at all, and she was wonderfully organised with the children. She just needed help lifting little 16-month-old Declan out of his cot, which I was more than happy to provide. We had a lovely time together, with me getting to know my new little granddaughter.

Just over a month later Ian and I were back in Wodonga as our youngest daughter Clare prepared for her second baby's birth. After my anxiety last time around, I must admit I was quietly relieved that Clare wanted me to look after Eva rather than be with her for the birth. Sometimes I think we midwifes know too much when it comes to our own children giving birth, and there's something to be said for leaving them to make their own way. It's certainly less stressful for the grandmother-to-be!

After a slow start, Clare's contractions hit in earnest and her daughter, Chloe, was born a few hours later, weighing an impressive 4.2 kilograms.

After a week with my new granddaughters it was time to return to Maningrida, and get back to helping other mothers and their babies. I'd almost finished my first day back at the clinic when I noticed a young girl of about 14 slumped on a chair in the corridor. At first I thought she was playing a game on her mobile phone, but ten minutes later as I walked back from the stockroom it struck me that something was wrong. She hadn't moved an inch and now I realised that she was just staring at the floor.

'Is someone looking after you?' I asked. She said nothing, clearly reluctant to meet my eye.

I asked a nurse if she knew who was caring for the girl.

'The doctor is talking to her mother,' she replied quietly. 'She was raped by four boys last night. From what I can gather she met one of them, and he took her to a place where the others were waiting. They held her captive for most of the night.'

I felt sick to the pit of my stomach and suddenly very protective of this poor, vulnerable girl. To give her some privacy I suggested she come and sit in my consulting room. When I came back with some tea for her, she was sitting on the bed, her face expressionless. She took the cup but still wouldn't meet my eye.

I asked her if she was in pain or bleeding and she shook her head. So I sat with her for a while and eventually she lay down on the bed and shut her eyes. I told her I'd be across the hall if she needed me, and left her to sleep. 'Leave light on' she said softly. I covered her with a blanket and crept quietly to the door. She asked me not to close it, so I pulled the privacy curtain, and took a last glimpse at this child, who had curled herself up in the foetal position on the bed. Her dishevelled hair had bits of dirt and dried leaves tangled in it.

That night I couldn't stop thinking about her and worrying about how she was going to deal with such a terrible ordeal. I found out the next day that she and her mother had gone to Darwin to meet with a worker from the Sexual Assault Referral Centre, who would support and help guide them through all the legalities and clinical testing required. I knew she was in good hands but I felt so desolate for her.

Almost a month later, Pam came to see me one Saturday morning, pale and close to tears.

'I got called out to an emergency last night,' she told me. 'A fourteen-year-old girl had committed suicide.'

Struggling to hold back her tears, Pam said she'd found the girl hanging lifeless in her bedroom.

'Beth, I had to cut her down,' she said in a choked voice. 'The family were crying and shouting at me to bring her back, but it was too late. There was nothing I could do. Every time I shut my eyes I see her. I can't get the sight out of my head.'

At first I didn't make the connection, but on Monday morning I discovered that the dead girl was the teenager we'd seen at the clinic. Heartbreakingly, she had decided her life was not worth living after what happened to her, and perhaps she felt no one cared.

No one was ever charged with her rape. I don't know if the boys were protected by their families, or if no charges could be laid due to insufficient evidence, but it was yet another tragic example of how far we have to go to improve our record on protecting children in the community. A recent report by the Australian Institute of Health and Welfare revealed that in 2012 rates of sexual assault among Aboriginal children were between two and four times higher than those for non-Aboriginal children in New South Wales, Queensland, South Australia and the Northern Territory.

Tragically this was not the first or last rape in the community and it concerned me deeply to think that the girls in my care were at such high risk. After that incident I redoubled my efforts to help warn the young girls at Ros's school to be mindful about going anywhere alone with boys. Teenagers in any community are vulnerable, but even more so in outback communities, where the grim reality is that rape is an endemic problem, not least because of child abuse that has affected generations of boys and girls.

One Saturday morning when I picked up Sheila for another of our regular hunting and gathering missions, I noticed she was using her stick and was noticeably thinner.

As usual I had no idea who else would be coming, but it was always a nice surprise to meet new women along the way. After picking up our companions for the day, Martha and two other women, we drove to Crab Creek. As Sheila rallied herself for a day of hunting she discarded her stick and set to work with her usual strength and energy.

Watching her while she worked, I was heartened to see that despite the cancer treatment she was still remarkably agile, crouching for long periods as she coaxed unsuspecting crabs out of their muddy hideaways. Heading back to the car, we met the other women, carrying buckets overflowing with long bums. Then we drove to our favourite spot at Rocky

Point, where the women unloaded a pile of wood ready for our feast. I gathered some dry grass and leaves to start a fire, and a bucketful of water to cook the shellfish.

We had a wonderful day and the memory of it became all the more precious because every time I saw Sheila after that she seemed to be getting thinner. She looked more and more frail, as though the cancer was eating her up – it was awful to see such a strong and vibrant person physically diminished like that, just as my parents had been.

Though I wanted to remain hopeful, I wondered how long my dear friend would manage to fight the malignancy of the disease.

Maningrida had been my home for three years by now, and in that time I'd seen plenty of fellow balandas come and go. Jobs out in the most remote areas of the bush, far away from the cities and bigger towns of Australia, often have a high turnover rate. Sometimes it's as simple as people not coping with the isolation and missing their families and friends, and the creature comforts many of us take for granted. Other times jobs in isolated areas can attract idealists who become disillusioned when they can't fulfil their dreams or their ideal of how things should be, or accept that some of the help they want to give isn't valued. But often in high-stress jobs, where you are dealing with life and death every day, many people eventually become burnt out by the trauma they experience day in and day out.

So when Pam told me she was leaving, I shouldn't have been surprised. She'd been in Maningrida almost two years, and loved the place, and her role within the community. She had great respect for the people she worked with, too, but she'd had a tough time recently and it had taken its toll. After discovering the body of the girl who suicided and having to cut her down, Pam had been through counselling, but I knew she'd never really got over the experience. That, combined with the horror of Nina's little girl's death and continual nights on call, had taken their toll. Both she and Glenn had agonised over their decision, but in the end she felt she had little choice but to start somewhere afresh.

Chapter 16
An incredible journey

As I gradually came to know more women in the community, I began to understand much more about their everyday lives and their needs. And I was filled with admiration for many of them, who endured difficult times with stoicism. I tried each day to do the best I could by each woman I saw. Some I knew I hadn't helped, and probably couldn't help. Others surprised me in their willingness to be open to some of the help and advice I offered, and inspired me with their resilience, their calm acceptance when life didn't go their way. I thought some of the mums I had worked with in Wodonga could have taken a leaf or two out of their books.

One day I had just delivered the fifth baby of a woman under my care, Kooreena. Her new daughter was a good size, and was feeding well, and once the tiny little mite had had her fill and been dressed up cosily, I took them both home. Koreena was chuffed because she and her baby were my first 'keepers' since I'd come to the community.

It was nightfall by the time we left the clinic, and Kooreena's house was in darkness. At first I assumed it was because no one was home. But she told me they didn't have electricity – one of the young men in their household had broken their power board with a stick during an argument. She seemed fairly calm about it all but I fetched a torch and gave her the clinic phone number in case she needed help overnight. I left her to it, confident that she and her baby would be just fine.

The following morning I was getting ready for work when I heard someone shouting my name. At the door I found Leona. 'Pet, Mel at Three Shelters has been leaking water,' she said. 'Now she's paining.'

We headed up to the shelters – three scruffy sheds with corrugated roofs and tents on the inside, not far from the clinic. They'd been built as temporary accommodation for people who lived on the outstations, for when they came into town shopping and visiting family, but some people had settled there permanently in tents.

I found Mel, a petite woman in her twenties, sitting on an upturned flour tin looking reassuringly relaxed. I'd been keeping a close eye on her in the past few months because she had gestational diabetes. She had been doing a great job of keeping it under control with a good diet, but a few weeks earlier I'd noticed that her baby bump was measuring a little less than it should for her gestation. I'd sent her for an ultrasound, which confirmed, to my relief, that though her baby was on the small side, the all-important blood flow to the foetus was normal.

With a little help, Mel managed to get into the car with me so I could take her to the clinic. We made her comfortable and she remained unaccountably calm, but as her contractions became gradually more intense she couldn't hide her pain.

Eventually I decided I'd better have a look to see what was going on, and was taken aback to see the baby's head already visible. I wrestled on a pair of protective gloves, inwardly cursing the unwieldy sterile material as Mel let out a strangled cry of pain. Suddenly the head was out! With one glove on and one off I caught the baby in the nick of time.

The little girl let out a hearty cry, kicking her legs and then nestling into her mother's chest. She seemed strong and well, but she weighed just 2 kilograms so she'd need to go to Darwin.

Once mother and baby were safely on the plane I drove to Kooreena's to check on her new arrival. I found her contented baby girl wrapped up in her bunny blanket, being looked after by her father, Mandu. As I gave the baby the once-over I saw Kooreena walking back from the shop, looking very sprightly despite being loaded with bags. It was clear that having a baby the day before was a mere a hiccup in her daily routine. I thought of all those articles in glossy magazines with tips from celebrities on bouncing back into shape after having a baby. Kooreena could teach them a thing or two.

The day after, a woman brought her 14-year-old daughter, Maiya, to see me and asked if I could give her a 'woman's check-up'. I knew that meant a pregnancy test. Maiya was dressed in a tight-fitting t-shirt and board shorts and she didn't look pregnant. I asked her when she'd had her last period.

'I don't know,' she muttered, fidgeting with embarrassment. 'But I'm not having sex.'

She gave me a urine sample, which I'd send off for an STI screening. Best to cover all bases. When she handed the container back, just to be sure, I carried out a pregnancy test on the liquid. My heart sank as two small stripes appeared on the strip – a positive result.

As soon as I delivered the results, her mother said without hesitation. 'We want the baby taken out.'

When I subsequently examined Maiya with the clinical ultrasound, I found she was about 19 weeks pregnant. Of course, this meant a termination was out of the question. I explained this gently and Maiya's mother stared at the screen angrily. Saying nothing, she turned her back on her daughter and tears began to roll down Maiya's face. I noticed in her history that she had presented to the clinic about seven months prior requesting an Implanon, but she'd been asked to return with a responsible guardian as she was under age.

Yet, after the initial shock of an unplanned, teenage pregnancy, Maiya adapted to her situation remarkably well. She listened to all my advice on the birthing process, how to care for herself and the baby and what to expect, with earnest concentration. When she came for her next appointment she was wearing a long skirt, which I knew indicated she was no longer a girl but a woman.

Maiya had not been attending school, but almost all the young girls I saw who became pregnant would then drop out of school. Although in Maningrida there are now facilities to make it easier for girls to return to education after the birth of a baby, I know of only one who has taken it up; the majority don't attend after they get pregnant, especially if there are no family members push them to.

In traditional Aboriginal society childhoods can be short and a girl is seen as physically able to become a bearer of children as soon as she gets to puberty. Education is generally not seen as something that's particularly useful for them.

In Maiya's case, as I'd seen so often, the father of her child wasn't involved. Her auntie became her support person, though Maiya would also often come to the clinic with a friend of similar age, and Maiya encouraged her to ask us for contraception and to bring along her guardian in order to be eligible for it.

In her third trimester Maiya's slight body stubbornly held her baby in a breech position, so in her final few weeks we had to send her to Darwin for a caesarean section, her auntie by her side.

She returned with a thriving baby boy, Aidan. The next time she was in the clinic, she asked me for the Implanon implant – she knew she'd have enough on her hands for a while with her little boy. So I was delighted that whenever I saw her she was managing brilliantly with him, as good if not better than many more experienced mums I have worked with over the years. Remarkable when you think that at that age lots of young girls have no responsibilities of their own at all.

✻

I was delighted to see Leona turn up at the clinic with Ceira and Jarrah one afternoon, and touched that when she saw me, Ceira broke free from her mother and came running towards me with her arms outstretched.

'My friend!' she proclaimed with a big smile as she clamped her arms around my legs.

The last time I'd seen Leona and her children, I'd been rushing to Kooreena's surprise labour. This time I made tea and as we chatted Leona breastfed 17-month-old Jarrah. I love the way Aboriginal mothers think nothing of feeding a child wherever they are. It's a natural part of mothering for them, as it should be for all of us. Many Aboriginal children continue to suckle until they're three years old and there are no taboos in them doing so, which I found very refreshing after all the resistance I'd encountered to breastfeeding in Victoria over the years.

His thirst quenched, Jarrah scrambled down again and began to totter around the room, fascinated by anything he could lay his little hands on. Before long I was wrestling a roll of surgical tape out of his mitts and attempting to distract him with a biscuit.

Somehow Leona and I got onto the subject of birthdays, and she told me that Ceira would soon be four. 'Pet, will you make birthday cake?' she asked me suddenly. 'A chocolate one!' she added with a grin.

In this community, children's birthdays mostly came and went with no recognition, so I was chuffed to have been asked and eager to fulfil Leona's request. I hadn't made a child's birthday cake since my own girls were little. On the anniversary of Ceira's birth I made a suitably gooey chocolate cake and sprinkled it with hundreds and thousands, then dropped it over to the family. I gathered from Leona it was a big hit!

It was my own birthday a few weeks later. I was driving through the community that day when I saw Nina lugging several bags of shopping on each arm. I pulled over and offered her a lift.

'Treaty' by Yothu Yindi started playing, and I turned up the radio. It was an anthem that had struck a chord with both black and white Australians, written in the early 1990s to protest Bob Hawke's failure to honour the promise he made at the Barunga Festival that the Australian government would at last recognise the rights of Aboriginal landowners. Hawke promised his government would sign a treaty to do so by 1990, but the promise wasn't fulfilled.

Soon the pair of us were singing along, belting out the lyrics: 'Treaty, yeah! Treaty, now!' at the top of our voices.

I turned into our street to witness a stunned elder jumping out of his skin at the sound of our caterwauling. Pulling to a stop we both collapsed into fits of giggles. After everything Nina had been through, it was so good to see her laugh.

✱

I had taken to driving up to the airport in the early mornings for some exercise away from the town's dogs. One morning as I drove home, I spotted a clinic ambulance outside Sheila's house.

I'd been to visit my friend just the evening before and it was clear she was going downhill rapidly. In the past few weeks her family had been caring for her at home, and the night before I'd found Sheila lying peacefully on a double bed with female members of her family sitting around her on mattresses on the floor, holding vigil. An older woman was stroking her hair while another gently rubbed her abdomen.

'Pet's here,' Rita, Sheila's granddaughter, said, beckoning me over.

As I sat on the edge of the bed, Sheila's eyes had flitted open. She reached out and I took her hand. I was so overcome with emotion I couldn't speak. Neither of us said anything but I hope she felt my concern and tenderness as I held her hand. Somehow I know she did. Sheila always had an uncanny knack for knowing how I was feeling. She was so thin and gaunt and I did wonder if this would be the last time I would see her alive.

I drove home to get Ian after seeing the ambulance, and we walked with heavy hearts to Sheila's house. As we approached, and the dogs' barking finally quietened down, my heart sank – I could hear wailing from inside. A clinic nurse appeared at the door. 'Beth, I'm sorry,' she said softly. 'She's gone.'

Ian put his arm around me and I told him I'd meet him at home. First I must pay my respects.

At the door I was met by Greta, Sheila's daughter. 'Come in and say goodbye, Pet,' she said.

Inside, I found six women sitting quietly on the floor – another daughter and five older women, who'd been with her all night. There were no men present. My friend was lying on the bed, veiled with a sarong and her face partially covered.

Greta encouraged me to sit on the bed and as I gingerly sat beside my friend, I thought about all our time together, tears streaming down my face. I was so grateful to be able to say goodbye for the last time; in fact, I still can't get over how generous the family were to let me join their circle and be with her at the end.

Before I left, I made sure to ask the women if they'd like us to close the clinic for the day as a sign of respect, but they said no. 'There are too many sick people and they need their medicine,' one said.

The following morning the family prepared to take the body to the airport, where it would be transported to the mortuary in Darwin, to allow time for relatives to arrive for the funeral. Some might take as long as six weeks to receive word of the death and make the journey to the community. Once everyone had arrived to mourn, my friend's body would be buried in a family plot either at her home or on country at an outstation.

A clinic ambulance was used as a hearse, with the women elders of the family in the back with the body, while the other family members walked behind. Some of the women had rubbed white ochre on their faces, arms and legs. Trailing the convoy were half a dozen vehicles packed full of men, women and children. The large turnout of mourners proved what I already knew – that my friend was immensely loved and respected by this community.

I joined the procession, walking the two kilometres to the airport, where a small charter plane was waiting. 'Would it be okay for me to go with the family on to the tarmac?' I asked one of the men as we approached the plane. I had to ask – suddenly I couldn't bear the idea of not seeing her right up to its doors, and I knew he'd tell me if it wasn't acceptable for me to go any further.

Thankfully he said it was fine so I continued on, and watched as the back doors of the vehicle were opened and the men of the family helped the women elders to climb down from the ambulance. As the rhythmical clicking of clap sticks filled the air and the mourners chanted, six men gently carried my friend onto the plane. Some of the women began crying and wailing and one of my friend's relatives threw herself violently to the ground. She did it again and again until two women came to her aid. They crouched on the ground and held her, sobbing together. I stood alongside them, choked with my own tears, giving in to the grief I felt.

Everyone moved off the tarmac to gather and watch as the plane taxied out, ready to take off. As it rose into the air, it was accompanied by a chorus of anguished cries and wailing. It was an extraordinary scene – the plane carrying my friend skywards as the cries of her loved ones resonated around us.

Once the plane had disappeared into the distance, people began to disperse, some in vehicles, some walking.

Not wanting to intrude, I dragged my feet behind the family. 'Pet, over here,' Rita called to me. I didn't have my stick and, she warned, there were cheeky dogs around. 'You walk with us at the front,' she said. Her kindness moved me so much I could only answer her with a grateful smile.

*

My friend's body was returned to the community for burial about six weeks later. When I saw groups of people heading to the family's home at sunset one evening I knew she must be back. I took up my dog stick and told Ian I was going to the funeral house.

When I arrived at the house, Rita ushered me into a dark room. Once my eyes had adjusted I could see some familiar faces – Greta was sitting quietly beside the closed coffin, which was draped with a light blanket. As I sat down next to her she reached over and held my hand.

'The morning that old lady passed away, there was a light came down from the sky and I knew she was gone,' she said.

I sat with her quietly for some time, thinking back on the happy memories my friend had left behind, but there was a gaggle of people waiting outside to pay their respects, so eventually I quietly took my leave and went out to join Rita on the porch as other mourners filtered in to say goodbye. High-pitched sounds of grief came from the room.

'You come back tomorrow night, Pet,' Rita said. 'There will be dancing.'

So the next night I returned. This time there were men playing didgeridoos, the low, mournful tones accompanied by the rhythmic beat of clap sticks. Outside the house two young men, painted with white ochre and dressed in loincloths, danced to the music as a huge orange moon rose in the east. The women of the household swayed along, scooping the air with their hands, pretending to gather shellfish to the rhythm.

Sadly I wasn't able to stay for her final burial – Ian and I had already booked tickets to travel home to Victoria for Easter. But when I returned to Maningrida, I went to visit her grave. After laying flowers there, I sat and thought how lucky I had been to know someone who had given me and so many others in the community so much, and who expected so little in return.

A few weeks later I took Greta and some of her friends out collecting pandanus and dye. When we got back we were met by Rita.

'Pet, did you get that car smoked?' she asked, referring to the Aboriginal ritual of using smoke to cleanse and send off spirits.

I felt worried – I hadn't.

Rita smiled. 'You know when you were picking up Mum?' she said. 'I thought I saw that old lady sitting in the back seat of your car. It was her spirit going with you to get pandanus.'

'That old lady can come with me any time,' I said, smiling.

Epilogue

When I first came to Maningrida I expected to last twelve months. Yet five years later I am struggling to think how I will tear myself away from the remote life. When my contract ends in June 2015 I know I will find it difficult to bid goodbye to the 36 women under my care and my friends in the community. I know I must because I am missing my own expanding family and the chance to see my grand-children grow up. But many of the people here have become like a family to me.

Of course, my time in Arnhem Land has not been without its challenges. Throughout my career I have learnt that midwifery is about so much more than 'delivering' babies.

It is about working in partnership with women and their families, and respecting and accepting a mother's knowledge and expertise, even if they differ from my own. Working in the far north, I've had to add to these the ability to understand some of our first people's cultural and spiritual beliefs.

Trying to do my best as a midwife for the mothers and children in the community can be hard sometimes. I see pregnant women with gestational diabetes who do not want to have their blood sugar levels checked, no matter what arguments I put forward. I see the diseases of poverty such as scabies and rheumatic heart disease, and I long for them to be obliterated. I treat fungal skin infections, and wish the people I care for would listen to my warnings about the dangers of dog excrement on the floor and cockroaches scuttling across the furniture.

But I have learnt that you have to be patient and try to take these things step by step. Sometimes, of course, that is easier said than done. However, I know that I can't afford for my frustration to overwhelm me. I came here to learn, to help people, and I like to think that I have been some use here. So, like many of my patients, I must learn to accept many things I can't change, and persevere.

One thing I know for sure is that every pregnant woman and new mother should have the expert care of a midwife, no matter where they are. Whether the women in my care want to take my advice is up to them. I can't force them to do things my way. I have learnt to accept that the value systems, ways of life and priorities of the women under my care in this community are entirely different to those of the women I treated for many years before coming up here. And I'm the one that's had to adapt to that and try to find ways of helping wherever I can.

Yet I can't help but take heart from the people I have won round, and who have won me round. I have met so many amazing, strong and admirable people in the community and when we stand side-by-side, wonderful things happen.

Having women like Nina and Jo at my side has made all the difference to my ability to get my message across. There is a growing push to encourage Aboriginal people to qualify as doctors, nurses, midwives and health professionals, but first more work needs to be done to encourage education and all the benefits it can bring. If we can do that, we can improve future health outcomes for whole families and ultimately the next generation. The major policy changes I must leave to our governments, whose efforts so far haven't been very successful. Perhaps that will change though. We can but hope. But in the meantime I know from my experience that we can all play our small part towards effecting major changes by learning to respect and understand each other better.

Nina tells me that, culturally, education is not viewed to be as important as family, and a lot of young women simply don't want to upset their elders by leaving the community to study. But I strongly believe knowledge is power in the best possible sense, so I am still doing my best to encourage young women to learn more by continuing to run classes like sexual health education at the school and helping to inform my young patients as best I can. I hope that by talking frankly and openly about sexual health issues, I will at the least help avert some unwanted teenage pregnancies, and empower these young girls to take their future into their own hands.

Always in the back of my mind is the fact that my time here is running out. I can only do the best I can in the short time I am here. But I am determined to make every day count.

For me, the women and children in my care remain a constant source of admiration and inspiration. I see mothers every day doing their best for their children, who are uncomplaining about the labour of childbirth and often back on their feet within hours, slaving away for their families.

It is an honour and a privilege to do my best for them, to give them the benefit of my experience not only as a midwife but as a wife and mother. My extended family of mothers and babies scattered across the land here are the reason I have loved every moment of my life as an outback midwife.

Loved the book?